George Tinworth

Frontispiece: Portrait of George Tinworth in old age.

George Tinworth

by Peter Rose

Chronology of Principal Works
Compiled by
Desmond Eyles

Harriman-Judd Collection
Volume I

Published by C.D.N. Corporation
Los Angeles, California, U.S.A. 1982

Copyright © 1982 Peter Rose and Desmond Eyles.
All rights reserved.
This book may not be reproduced, in whole or in part, in any form (except by reviewers for the public press), without written permission from the authors or publishers.

Library of Congress Catalogue Card Number 82-072976.
International Standard Book Number 0-9609320-0-3

Designed by Carolyn Kinsey and Allen Harriman and set in Times Roman.
Printed in Los Angeles by Industrial Printers of California.

Published in America by Coin Dealer Newsletter, Inc., Los Angeles.

Table Of Contents

	PAGE
Introduction and Acknowledgements	7-8
List of Black and White Plates	9

The Life and Work of George Tinworth:
    1. 1843-1866: Childhood and Early Training 11-19
    2. 1867-1883: Doulton & Co.; Making a Reputation 21-33
    3. 1884-1897: Achievement and Maturity 35-43
    4. 1897-1913: Decline and Final Years 45-53
    5. Assessment and Appreciation 55-60

Notes 61

**Catalogue of the Harriman-Judd Collection of
Sculpture and Pottery by George Tinworth:**
    Introduction 63
    Section I: Early Decorated Pottery 64
    Section II: Middle Period Pottery 65-69
    Section III: Late Period Pottery 70-71
    Section IV: Religious Panels 71-75
    Section V: Animal Groups 76-82
    Section VI: Human Figures and Groups 82-85

Colour Plates 87-150

Chronology of Principal Works by George Tinworth 153-188

Identification Marks on George Tinworth Pottery and Sculpture 189

Bibliography 191-193

Index 195-198

Fig. 1. Oval Plaque: Self-portrait of George Tinworth *(Harriman-Judd Collection)*

Introduction and Acknowledgements

The collection from which the catalogue section of this book derives is the creation of Allen Harriman and Edward Judd. Its scope extends through late nineteenth century into recent twentieth century English studio and art pottery, with a major interest shown in the products of the firm of Doulton & Co. The collection is, however, by no means confined to pottery alone, as a parallel interest in nineteenth and twentieth century European and American paintings has developed along side it. Both major areas of collecting are being actively extended; it is consequently a particularly challenging task to settle upon any one aspect in order to form a catalogue. The group of sculpture and pottery decorated by George Tinworth is not only one of the most established sections of the collection but is undoubtedly the largest and most varied concentration of his work assembled. It is, therefore, appropriate that he should be the subject of the first volume of a series of works based on the collection.

Although the first piece of Doulton pottery was purchased in about 1960 from a Los Angeles dealer, it was almost a decade before any substantial increase in the collection occurred. Visits to Europe in the 60's had stimulated interest in the English revival of salt-glazed stoneware and gradually further pieces were purchased. In the early and mid-seventies in both Europe and America there occurred a major re-assessment of the late nineteenth century art and studio potters, and collectors of these began to multiply. The process was further stimulated by a series of exhibitions organised by Richard Dennis, accompanied by comprehensive catalogues, books and other publications (notably by Desmond Eyles, Geoffrey Godden, Malcolm Haslam and others). Dealers specialising in the field became established, and the increased market value of the pots drew out major pieces from the attics and cellars of private owners.

It was not, however, until the mid-seventies that Allen Harriman and Edward Judd, having moved to their present residence, were able to devote the time and resources necessary to capture, in an extremely volatile market, the major pieces which now make the collection pre-eminent. Every serious collector knows how essential it is to be in the right place at the right time in order to secure first quality examples for his collection. Sales catalogues have to be closely studied, specialist dealers alerted, contacts of all kinds developed, but, most essential of all, qualitative judgment has to be exercised. To most people it might seem a daunting undertaking to engage in such activities several thousand miles away from England, the main centre of activity in the field. Allen Harriman and Edward Judd, however, seized on the new ease with which travellers could cross the Atlantic, and the instant contact of the trans-Atlantic telephone call, and successfully secured many major pieces of the highest quality in each of their rapidly extending fields of interest.

When the collection is the joint achievement of two individuals, it is of some interest to understand the respective roles played by each. It is significant that the partners in the collection hold distinct, different, and occasionally contradictory views; often disagreeing, but performing essentially complementary and supportive roles, resulting in a formidable joint perception and judgment.

The ceramic collection now extends over the whole range of English late nineteenth and twentieth century pottery. The work of all the major Doulton artists is represented by many pieces of the highest quality. Second to Doulton is the work of the Martin Brothers and, in particular, the grotesques of Robert Wallace Martin. There are large groups also of Moorcroft, Pilkington Royal Lancastrian, Minton, Della Robbia, and the modern studio potters, Lucie Rie, Hans Coper and Elizabeth Fritsch. These, it is hoped, will form the subject of later volumes in the series.

The decision to make the collection of Tinworth's sculpture and pottery the nucleus of a comprehensive survey of his life and works has provided the author with a long wished for opportunity to evaluate thoroughly Tinworth's artistic worth. It is, therefore, to Allen Harriman and Edward Judd that he would wish to extend his grateful thanks for accepting the very considerable financial outlay involved in such an ambitious project.

The work, life and character of George Tinworth have fascinated nineteenth century pottery enthusiasts for many years. Foremost amongst them is Desmond Eyles, who has given Tinworth detailed attention in several of his works. It was his intention to publish a full length life of the sculptor potter, and he had assembled much original material towards that goal, when the prospect of the present work persuaded him to contribute the "Chronology of Principal Works" instead. Of equal importance, however, has been his enthusiastic support for the project and his generosity in making available to the author the wealth of material, notes, etc. which he had assembled over the years. His help throughout has been invaluable.

The present intense collecting interest in the products of the Doulton pottery firm owes much to Richard Dennis, whose exhibitions have been a great stimulus to an ever widening public. He has provided not only many of the objects in the collection but he has given throughout wholehearted support to the project. His enthusiasm has been invaluable.

The author would like to thank the following for their assistance in gathering information and providing advice: Paul Atterbury; Jimmy Cox; Roger Few; Judy Fox; Albert Gallichan; Louise Irvine; John Jenkins; Jocelyn Lukins; Stephen Nunn; Lt. Col. (Ret'd) R.W. Nye; Harry Ogle; David Robinson; Jessica Rutherford; Clive Wainwright; Charles York.

With the exception of some of the black and white illustrations, which were supplied by Royal Doulton Tableware Ltd., the Victoria and Albert Museum and the Smithsonian Institution, all the photographs were specially taken by Graham Miller who has devoted meticulous care in ensuring a consistently high standard. Thanks are also due to the two secretaries, Stella Gammon and Veronica Symons, who managed to successfully unravel much confused and complex manuscript material.

Desmond Eyles would like to acknowledge the help of the following in compiling the "Chronology of Principal Works". W.J. Carey, R. Dennis; W. Fairhall; Revd. B. Giles; Revd. E.C. Hamlyn; A.W. Heywood; F.W. Kerry; A. Leigh; Miss F. Lovering; Revd. A. Owens; Revd. W.V. Pitts; Revd. K.V. Povey; Revd. J. Rutherford; B. Saunders, J. Shorter, Revd. C.A. Woale.

Both the author and Desmond Eyles wish to thank the following institutions for their unfailing help: Brighton Museum and Art Gallery; Brighton Polytechnic; City Museum and Art Gallery, Stoke-on-Trent; Cuming Museum, London S.E.17; Minet Library, London S.E.5; Museum of Applied Arts and Sciences, Sydney, N.S.W.; Royal Academy, London; Royal Army Chaplaincy Museum, Bagshot; Royal Doulton Tableware Ltd.; Royal Scottish Museum, Edinburgh; Smithsonian Institution, Washington, D.C.; Southwark Local Studies Library, London S.E.22; Victoria and Albert Museum, London.

List of Black and White Plates

Frontispiece: Portrait of George Tinworth in old age.

Fig. 1. Oval Plaque: Self-portrait of George Tinworth. (*Harriman-Judd Collection*)

Fig. 2. Drawing from memory of George Tinworth's birthplace.

Fig. 3. Terra-cotta plaque: *"The Wheelwright's Shop"*, 1877.

Fig. 4. Canon Gregory: a page from George Tinworth's autobiography.

Fig. 5. A page from a Doulton & Co. catalogue illustrating medallions by George Tinworth.

Fig. 6. Cabinet, 1871: designed by Charles Bevan with plaques by George Tinworth. (*Victoria and Albert Museum*, London).

Fig. 7. Jug: Philadelphia Exhibition, 1876. (*Smithsonian Institution*, Washington).

Fig. 8. Terra-cotta panel: *"The Release of Barabbas"*.

Fig. 9. The York Minster panel: a page from George Tinworth's autobiography.

Fig. 10. The Guards' Chapel Lunettes. Two panels illustrated in the 1883 catalogue.

Fig. 11. Fountain: Paris Exhibition, 1878.

Fig. 12. Mrs. Tinworth's diary. March 4-March 10, 1888.

Fig. 13. The Shaftesbury Memorial: a page from George Tinworth's autobiography.

Fig. 14. Terra-cotta panel. Morley College, 1889.

Fig. 15. George Tinworth working on the model of the Fawcett Monument, 1892-93.

Fig. 16. The Spurgeon Memorial: a page from George Tinworth's autobiography.

Fig. 17. Sir Henry Doulton: a page from George Tinworth's autobiography.

Fig. 18. *"Noah Constructing his Ark"*: a page from George Tinworth's autobiography.

Fig. 19. Terra-cotta panel: *"All Misery Past"*.

Fig. 20. Terra-cotta panel: *"The Greek Mother"*.

Fig. 21. Portrait of George Tinworth working on the model for the Shakespeare Monument.

Fig. 22. Terra-cotta panel: The Doulton Artists, 1876.

Fig. 23. *"The Sowing of Tares"*. An unused lunette illustrated in the 1883 catalogue. (*Royal Army Chaplaincy Museum*, Bagshot).

Fig. 24. Terra-cotta panel: *"Going to Calvary"*.

Fig. 25. Terra-cotta panel: *"Edward the Fourth Meeting Lady Gray"*.

Fig. 26. Portrait of George Tinworth working on the terra-cotta panel: *"Christ before Herod,"* 1887.

Fig. 27. Terra-cotta panel: *"The Taming of the Shrew"*.

Fig. 28. Clay sketches for panels on the Shakespeare Moument (Contemporary photographs in the *Southwark Local Studies Library*).

The Life and Work of George Tinworth

Chapter One

1843-1866 Childhood and Early Training

George Tinworth, a sculptor of great natural talent, achieved fame despite a childhood spent in poverty and deprivation. As a young man he was given an art training in one of the newly established government schools of design, with much encouragement and support from an outstanding teacher. Throughout his career as a sculptor he occupied a secure and privileged position in a large and prosperous commercial company owned by the Doultons, a family of enlightened industrialists. His output of sculpture and pottery was prodigious, both in scale and quantity, receiving much critical and public acclaim from the start of his working life.

Although at the height of his fame he was visited regularly by royalty, leading members of church and state, distinguished literary figures and the most eminent of critics, he remained close to his humble origins in speech and thought. Wide acknowledgement of the vitality and skill of his terra-cotta sculpture resulted in many public commissions in churches, on public buildings and in parks, but above all in a long and triumphant series of international exhibitions.

It might be asked why such a man is not now firmly placed alongside the recognised masters of nineteenth century art and sculpture — for no account of Tinworth will be found in twentieth century works of general art history and criticism. Tinworth's reputation is at present secure within the specialist field of late nineteenth century "art pottery", but it extends no further. The present day neglect of Tinworth by art historians indicates that the task of re-evaluating his general artistic worth is still awaited.

The general reappraisal of art and design in the last half of the nineteenth century which is now taking place allows for a cooler, less emotionally charged response to its artifacts. Together with this change of view, present day attitudes to hierarchies in art and indeed in the categorisation of what constitutes an art form have shifted significantly. George Tinworth, a master craftsman who aspired to be a pure artist in the traditional sense, is now entitled to a serious examination in the context of more general art criticism.

George Tinworth's art and character were formed from a volatile mixture of ingredients. In childhood, lack of basic education and extreme family poverty were joined to fierce religious conviction and a sturdy working-class pride. Pride tempered by humility characterises many of the episodes in his life recounted in his unpublished autobiography, written in the last few years of his life and extensively used in this study.[1]

An episode from his later years when he was aged fifty four, with his major work completed, describes such an occasion. He had been made an Officer of the Academy by the French Government in 1876 in recognition of his services to "public instruction and the Universal Exhibition".[2] He had taken to wearing the Rosette of the order while travelling in France on his second visit, after the death of Sir Henry Doulton. He was self-conscious about this rather ostentatious gesture and suspected people of ridiculing him. He decided on impulse to see whether his name was listed among the members of the Academy. To his chagrin he discovered that it was not: "So I paid a guide to take me to the Government Offices to know about it. They said foreign members were not put in, but Tadamar's (sic) name was down and Mr. Gosse

so I took it out of my coat and I have never worn it since, and I feel none the worse for it. The English want no favour, only justice and true liberty."

The first account of his early career appeared in 1883 when Tinworth was aged forty. The occasion was an exhibition of his sculptural work at a gallery in Conduit Street, London. The Fine Art Society published a lavishly illustrated vellum bound volume containing a piece on the artist and an evaluation of his work by Edmund Gosse.[3] Although many accounts have since been written about him whom Gosse described as the "man who has been lifted by the force of his own genius out of the poorest class, and who has become a distinguished artist without ceasing to be an artisan," most were based on Gosse's original work. In 1975, however, Desmond Eyles published a more intimate and authentic impression[4] drawing on additional material which had come to light, notably Tinworth's own autobiography.

The account which follows adopts the more realistic, less idealised approach, for there is evidence that, for all the fine writing in the Gosse piece, an element of romantic embroidering was allowed to colour the sparse facts at the author's disposal. A letter from Tinworth to Gosse demonstrates some of his difficulties in gathering materials from the direct source. The letter, dated August 10th, 1882, is written not in Tinworth's stumbling and largely illiterate hand but in the regular and assured writing of his wife, Alice, whom he had married the previous year and who faithfully recorded his memories. Although extending to six pages, it is completely unstructured with much useful information scattered in disorderly confusion. He ends the letter: "I am afraid I have said too much already concerning myself, but you know how to make short of it. I hope I have not put you to much inconvenience in not writing before."

George Tinworth was born on the 5th of November, 1843, at No. 6 Milk Street, Walworth in South London (fig. 2). His childhood and early manhood was spent in Walworth, Lambeth and Stockwell, areas which had already

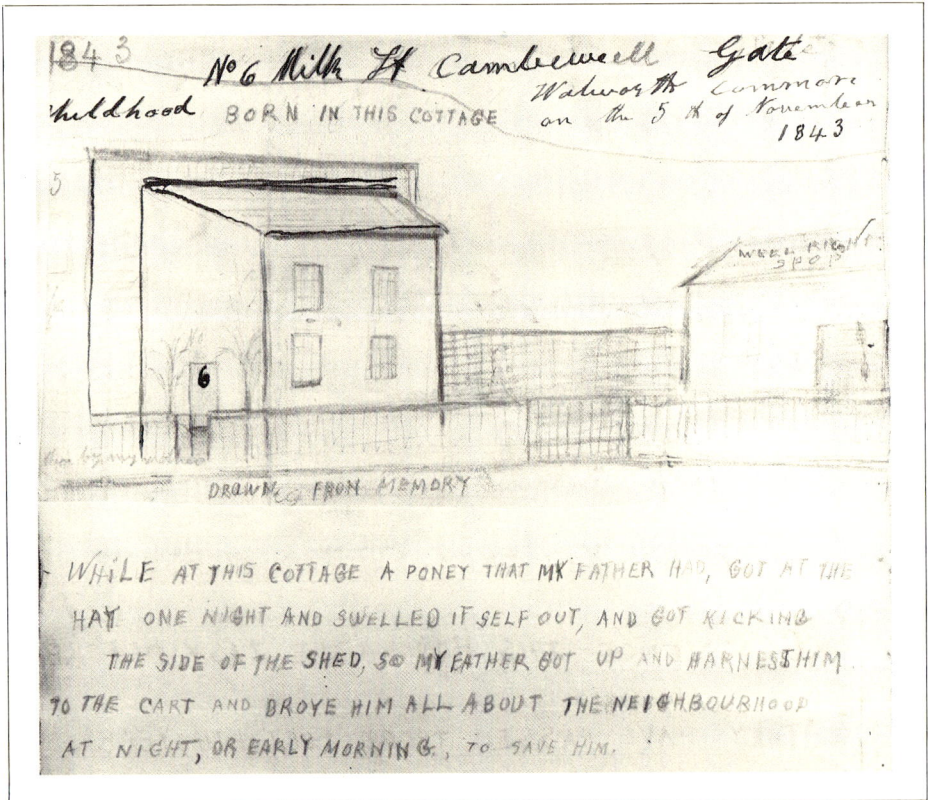

Fig. 2. Drawing from memory of George Tinworth's birthplace.

degenerated from their pre-Industrial Revolution charm to become that disorderly amalgam of factories, offices and terraced houses which survives to this day, even after much destruction of property during the 1939-45 war and post-war re-building. His parents were ordinary working class folk — his father Joshua a greengrocer turned wheelwright, his mother Jane a shop assistant in a pastrycooks. They met in George Clayton's Dissenters' Chapel and both shared the extreme fundamentalist faith which had such a crucial influence on George Tinworth's art.

The family fortunes, always shaky, degenerated further during George Tinworth's childhood. Real poverty reduced their lives to a dull grind of seemingly endless work for little reward. Food, warmth and the many creature comforts taken for granted by the poorest in the community today were frequently inadequate.

In spite of much suffering and discomfort, Tinworth's childhood was not an unhappy one. His mother, fortified by an impregnable faith, gave him unwavering support. His father, portrayed by Gosse as a drunken brute, was, according to Tinworth's own account, a man of character and pride and "a grand man when he was sober "."To show further what sort of man my father was, when he was hard up he and mother were invited to a relative's house to dinner, and when they were sitting down to dinner my uncle was silly enough to say 'I will give poor Josh a dinner!' Then my father jumped up and said 'D--m your dinner' and he and mother left the house at once."

In many ways Tinworth resembled his father; he appreciated and shared in his humour. Much of the autobiography concerns his father's life and episodes from George Tinworth's own childhood: the language and presentation are startlingly direct and fresh, although idiosyncratic in spelling and grammar. The extracts from it used in this account have been corrected for the more routine errors, but at the same time, retaining as far as possible the flavour of the original. The facsimile pages reproduced provide an indication of the scale of that task.

Stories told by his father made a deep impression on him. In 1825 his father was working as a slater's assistant on the roof of St. Catherine's Docks. "One day one of the slaters, a practical joker, nailed my father down to the roof by his coat and trousers, so when this man had gone below one of the labourers came and released him. Then my father got the slater's overcoat and spread it out on the roof and nailed it down in the same way. When the man came up again he saw what had been done to his coat and found out who had done it. He chased my father over the roof to the last gutter. He thought he had got him, but there was a scaffold pole left standing a few feet away from the building in the river and my father jumped for it and slid down to the bottom and it so frightened the man that he called for him to come up and said he would forgive him."

Tinworth's father Joshua had two brothers and three sisters. They lived in Kennington where Joshua's mother kept a laundry, having moved from Essex where his father had been a landscape gardener to the gentry. Piety and biblical erudition were much in evidence — his sisters were named Jamima, Kezia and Kerenhappuch after the three daughters of Job.

The parents of George Tinworth's mother, Jane Daniel, lived very appropriately in Lion Street, Walworth. Her father worked for a Mr. Hack, a carpenter who lived nearby. Here also Protestant Christianity was a dominant factor, for Mr. Hack was preacher at the local chapel. The family, like so many in the early nineteenth century, had moved from the country to the town in search of work. George Tinworth recalls that "my mother often told me about my grandmother Compton's home at Mitcham and the lavendar fields there, but I did not take notice of what she said."

From the start, George Tinworth's mother was noted for her piety; people called her the "young Quakeress". She had lived for a while with her aunt in Rochester, Kent. The aunt, a widow, had been "turned out" of the Baptist Chapel for remarrying too soon after the death of her first husband. However, the Chapel relented and allowed her back in after re-baptism. She guarded Jane's virtue ferociously and would say to her in chapel "read that Miss (the hymn 'Come ye sinners, poor and wretched') and don't get garping about."

After her marriage, a succession of deaths in infancy preceded George's birth. He was the fourth male child — but the first to survive. His mother told him before she died that "she made the same vow that Samuel's mother made, that was, to lend me to the Lord when I was born, if I should live. Well, I did live and she tried to keep her vow, but in time I got out of her control and went my own way, but no razor has ever come upon my head, so part of her vow has been kept."

Although fundamentalist Christian beliefs were the key to George Tinworth's character and ideas, from the start his natural high spirits carried him away from strict and joyless piety. There were visits to the fair at Camberwell Green where he watched dramatic performances and tried to draw them on a slate that his mother had bought him. Later he recalls visiting a fair and climbing on the wheel of the van to peer through a crack behind the theatre thus observing Clown, Pantaloon and Columbine on and off stage.

His father, said to be "the most industrious man about the neighbourhood 'till disappointment came,' " lost his greengrocery business at the time of the Irish Famine in 1845 and set up as a wheelwright. But failure dogged him. A machine he constructed to aid his business failed to work, but he converted it into a barrow for George with the wheel from the machine incorporated into it. The young George loved his wheelbarrow but "my father took to the drink and so went down and we with him. He took my wheelbarrow from me and sold it to a shopkeeper for his boy. I never forgot the boy that had my barrow. He is an old man now and I know him still, although it is sixty years ago."

George, at the age of seventy, remembered vividly his beleaguered family with the broker's man[5] lurking outside the house, and being instructed by his mother not to open the door so as to allow the man to get in. But he did get in, to be confronted by George's father in drunken fury jabbing a pointed fork in the table between them.

They moved to a small house in Locks Fields, Walworth, with a wheelwright's shop nearby. There was a temporary improvement in their fortunes and George was given money by his father — the first sixpence he had ever possessed. He had seen two china figures in a pawn-shop and when he produced his sixpence the pieces were sold to him. "It would be a good thing for art if the children of rich men could be trained to love art, and buy art objects when young" the old George Tinworth declared, no doubt thinking of the many unsold sculptures gathering dust in his studio.

On a Christmas morning George remembered marching out with his father to claim an unpaid debt so that they could buy food for their Christmas dinner. They obtained the money, persuaded a shopkeeper to open his shop and to sell them the ingredients for his mother to make six small Christmas puddings as there was not enough time to cook a large one. " 'Now', my father said to me, 'you can tell the boys you have had six Christmas puddings this Christmas'. "

George Tinworth recalls many tales of his father's wit and spirit and his unquenched pride. He would send George into the chandler's shop to "lend us two loaves on trust". If they refused, he would go back to that shop when he had money in his pockets, order a great quantity of groceries, all of which had to be individually weighed and packaged and then, when all had been finally wrapped, would say "Let me see, I have made a mistake. I have come to the wrong shop. You would not let my boy have two loaves the other day. I

Fig. 3. Terra-cotta plaque: *"The Wheelwright's Shop"*, 1877.

cannot buy anything of you." He refused to complete a job for a man who allowed himself to be henpecked by his wife who was continually giving instructions over his shoulder. He said to George, "Put up the tools, we will have no more of this job", and he told the man to take off his trousers and give them to his wife for she was the one to wear them!

Tinworth's first experience of work outside the family business was in a fireworks factory. He nearly blew himself and fellow passengers on the Peckham Horse Omnibus to pieces when two brown paper bags containing fourteen pounds of gunpowder leaked into the basket in which he was carrying them; fortunately no-one was smoking nearby. High spirits brought his job to an abrupt end when George and two companions, on the way to work, discovered a congealed mass of treacle spilled on the pavement. One of the other boys slapped treacle on young George's face and received payment in kind, with the result that all three arrived at work covered in treacle — and were immediately sacked.

At the age of fourteen, George began work at a hot pressers in Watling Street in the City. His working day was from seven in the morning until nine o'clock at night, each day including Saturday. He was paid four shillings for an eighty-four hour week. He would travel from home with slices of bread and butter and a penny in his pocket. Returning home on Saturday night with his four shillings wages, he could not resist buying a "nigger boy made of india rubber" for twopence. However, after three weeks he had enough; he returned to assist his father in the wheelwright's shop.

Misfortune still dogged the family; thieves broke into the shop and stole the tools, and these had to be painstakingly replaced by searching the local pawn-shops for cheap substitutes. While assisting his father, George contrived to experiment with wood carving when his father was out; a boy assistant keeping a look-out for his return (fig. 3). If this should happen unexpectedly, he would pull his carving from the vice and fling it into a distant corner of the workshed. Occasionally he would show his father what he had done; the response was characteristic: "Ah, my boy, you may thank me for that, and you have got enough wood in your head to make another one." However, he was delighted with an imitation pistol made by George which was polished with black lead to increase its seeming authenticity. Joshua took it into the tap room of his local public house, pointed it at a man he knew, crying out:"I said I would do it for you and now I will." The man was sufficiently deceived by the imitation pistol to plead: "Don't be a fool, no, don't be a fool, Josh." His mother, on the other hand, was consistently encouraging and it was through her showing a local master plasterer the figure of Samuel which George had carved that the first suggestion that he ought to go to Art School was made.

Tinworth's discovery of the Lambeth School of Art in Millers Lane, and in particular his meeting with the distinguished head-master John Sparkes, marked a moment of destiny in his career. A whole new world of experience and opportunity sprang to life, rapidly transforming the poor ignorant boy into a celebrity.

The story was told and retold throughout Tinworth's career and finally (and, it must be assumed, definitively) was set down in his own life story. His own words vividly recapture the occasion. Armed on the first visit with the copy in wood of the infant Samuel from a plaster cast already referred to (or, according to Gosse in his 1883 account, "a little head of Garibaldi — copied from a print in a newspaper"), and accompanied by a young companion, he sought and found the newly established art studios of the Lambeth School of Art in Millers Lane, Lambeth. "I saw an old lady going into the school and she invited me in. When I got inside and saw the statues and water-colour portraits from the model that the students had done,I felt in a new world. I told this woman if I had the stone I could carve the statues before us. I did not know the grandeur of the antique then as I do now. I asked her if I could come and be taught art work. So I thought I would come and see Mr. Sparkes the head-master. So I went the next night and a boy lifted me up to look through the window and Percy Ball was modelling from one of the statues with hardly anybody there. It was modelling night and I said if there were no more people in the room the next night I would go in. The next night I had another lift up to look in. It was full of people, as it was painting night. I had brought the bust of Handel that I had carved in Portland Stone at Hope Street. I had carved it in my lap. I went round to the side door and Mr. Sparkes was coming out and I showed it to him. Someone must have told me who he was. I asked him if I could come and be taught modelling and he said come in and see what we are doing and introduced me to Mr. Ball the modelling master saying 'Here's a new student for you, Mr. Ball'. So that was all right, but how was I to get the four shillings to pay the entrance fee? My mother got it from somewhere. We did not tell my father anything about it until a long time afterwards, then I had to tell him for he said 'I give you money but you never have got any '."

There is another independent account of the early days or, strictly, evenings spent at Lambeth School of Art. Robert Wallace Martin, the most talented and eccentric of the four brothers who later formed the Martin Brothers pottery, was a fellow pupil and befriended Tinworth. He recalls: "It was upon one of these occasions a rough looking youth timidly presented himself, perhaps I ought not to say rough for there was nothing low about him though poor and hard worked, he was evidently a young genius and soon tried an original panel 'The Roman Soldier Mocking Christ'. We became great friends and walked home together as we both lived in Walworth and he had to pass my parents' door which soon after opened to let him in and he became a welcome guest."[6]

Robert Wallace Martin had a studio in his home and sometimes in the holidays would let George copy the back of the model he was working from.

ABOUT THIS TIME CANON GREGORY WAS VICAR 45
OF ST MARYs THE LESS IN THE PRINCES ROAD.
CANON GREGORY WAS THE STARTER OF THE ART SCHOOL IN PRINCES ROAD. THEN IT WAS MOVED TO MILLERS LANE KING EDWARD WHEN PRINCE OF WALES LAID THE FOUNDATION STONE, THE SCHOOL STANDS ON A PART OF VAUXHALL GARDENS. THAT WAS

I HEARD HIM SAY HE THOUGHT THAT SOME OF THE NAMES OF THE STUDENTS OF THE LAMBETH ART SCHOOL SHOULD BE RETTEN ON ON THE WALLS OF OF THE SCHOOL,

IT AS BEEN SAID THAT CANON GREGORY WAS THE BEST ICHARMAN THEY HAD KNOWN;

HE WAS A NICE MAN AND HIS SISTER WAS LIKE HIM.

A FEW YEARS AGO HE TOOK ME UP TO THE ROOF OF ST PAULS TO SEE THE MEN PLACING THE MOSARE ON THE CEILING, AND WHEN WE WAS COMING OUT HE TOLD ME, WHEN EVER HE WAS GOING IN, THERE WAS ALL WAYS SOME ONE COMEING OUT OR GOING IN.

CANON GREGORY 40 YEARS AGO

I DO NOT KNOW WHAT HE EVER SAID TO ME WHEN I USED TO GO UP TO RECEIVE ANY THING FROM HIS HANDS IN THE SHAPE OF MEDALS. OR PRIZES STUDENTS ARE TO CONFUSED AT THE MOMENTS, THERE WAS A STUDENT AT THE R.A. BEFORE I CAME THERE THAT TOOK ALL THE MEDELS AND PRIZES, BUT NOTHING WAS HEARD OF HIM AFTER WARDS, SO IT IS NOT A SIGN WHAT YOU ARE GOING TO BE IF YOU GET MEDALS.

Fig. 4. Canon Gregory: a page from George Tinworth's autobiography.

Although they later went to the Royal Academy Schools together, the friendship ended — probably as a result of the rivalry between the Martin Brothers and Doulton's. Tinworth later denied that he "owed a lot to Martin" or that they worked together all night at Millers Lane — no doubt a reference to Gosse's highly romanticised account of their friendship.

Both Tinworth and Martin were extremely fortunate to have discovered the Lambeth School of Art and, in particular, the highly talented and enlightened teacher John Sparkes. The School had been founded in 1854 by Canon Gregory (fig. 4) to enable "the parishioners of Lambeth to obtain an elementary knowledge of design."[7] As the teaching was entirely done in the evenings, it shared the premises of the National School in Princess Road. This proved inconvenient as all the clutter of the practical art class had to be cleared away at the end of each session for the School to function the following day. Therefore, in 1860, John Sparkes contrived to get special rooms for the classes in Millers Lane. The following year Tinworth became a pupil and, night after arduous night, struggled with the laborious process of becoming a competent sculptor.

John Sparkes played a vital part in training and later in establishing Tinworth at Doulton's. His distinguished teaching career extended from 1856, when he took over the recently formed Lambeth School of Arts, until 1898, when he retired from the position of Head Teacher at the Central Government Art School at South Kensington (later to become the Royal College of Art). *The Times* obituary[8] described him as "for many years the most prominent art teacher in the country." Undoubtedly the progress of art education in England owed much to him. In a series of reports to government committees he advocated many enlightened reforms, several so far-sighted that a century later some still remain unrealised. His own teaching strength was in sculpture and, even after his appointment to the South Kensington School, he continued to guide the Lambeth School. He taught a distinguished group of sculptors — including H. Bates, F.W. Pomeroy, G.J. Frampton, W. Goscombe John, J. Swan and A. Drury, as well as many eminent painters. Through friendship and persistence he persuaded Henry Doulton to start up an Art Pottery at Lambeth, which provided Tinworth with the life-long opportunity of practising as a sculptor.

Art and design education in England at that time relied heavily on a system of graded tests and centrally judged examinations. The salary of the art master depended upon the success of his pupils in these tests and therefore encouraged attitudes which today would be anathema to any aspiring artist or designer. Wallace Martin, although successful, attacked this system perceptively and with characteristic rebelliousness, but Tinworth undertook the seemingly endless challenges of prizes and medals to be won with a more passive acceptance. Indeed, he relished the triumphs and even suffered the disappointments with gusto.

In December of 1864 he was admitted to the Schools of the Royal Academy, having presented a Hercules modelled under the direction of Sparkes. Tinworth describes a particular competition he won while at Lambeth: "After I had been there for some time I tried for the £2 prize. I designed a panel of 'The Savior being Mocked by the Soldiers'. I could not afford a model so I got my brother Tom at home to sit for it. Sometimes I stood myself. I carted it about from Hope Street to Lambeth School and from school back to Walworth. My brother Charlie brought the panel in clay one night. When there was a model sitting you had to go to the other door those nights. But larkish students from the other school told my brother to kick hard and he wore clogs at that time. I was in the drawing class in the same room and the noise of his kicking sounded very loud inside. The attendant ran out and so did I. Well, I got the two pound prize with it. To pay my school fees

I used to have to pawn my Sunday coat."

At the Royal Academy, Tinworth faced tougher competition and experienced failure as well as success. He also had to attend morning as well as evening sessions. His father, by this time somewhat reconciled to his son's artistic career, was finally won round: "When I got into the Royal Academy I had to tell my father about it as I had to go in the mornings to do my probationership from ten to one o'clock. So I asked one morning if he could spare me and he said I might go. When I got home at dinner time my mother was crying with pleasure which made me feel like doing the same. So every morning I went early to the shop, I did a bit of work then home to breakfast, then to the Royal Academy till one o'clock. Then I walked back to work. On lecture night I had to do the journey twice in one day. No money to ride. I did this for a long time."

After winning a silver medal for a life study which was highly commended by the President of the Academy, he decided to enter for the gold medal. The cost was considerable, he spent all his savings on hiring models and, in addition, Mr. Sparkes with characteristic generosity gave him ten pounds. Unfortunately, he won nothing and at last was provoked into criticising the system. "I hardly know what to think of this medal business. It is not worth anything to an artist. You cannot wear the medals if you gain them. If you were a boot maker you might show them in your window. They do no good to the student if he gets one but the disappointment if he does not get one I think shortens his life for him. . . . I think the judges ought to think more of the original part of a work of art than of the mechanical side or the fine finish. I think instead of giving medals it would be better to give them a five pound note to put in the Post Office Savings Bank."

His tutors at the School were drawn from the Academicians, a good system, which still continues. He mentions several prominent artists who tutored him: "I learned more from Mr. Weekes[9] than I did from any other Academicians for he would take a bit of clay and do a bit for you on your life study. Foley[10] would take a tool and cut any work to show me where I was wrong, but Weekes would mend it. Foley told me there was as much in a hand as there was in the whole figure." It was Weekes, however, who said to him the encouraging words about his ambitions: "You will do it because you stick to it."

Models play a large part in his memories of the years at the School. Some were clearly great characters and he recalls one that, having drunk more than was wise, fell off the throne and rising unsteadily to his feet remarked: "I think, sir, I am a little out of position."

Chapter Two

1867-1883 Doulton & Co.; Making A Reputation

The years 1866 and 1867 brought together the two events which determined George Tinworth's life-time working circumstances. His long and arduous apprenticeship in the art of sculpture reached fulfilment when a plaster group of figures was exhibited at the highly competitive and prestigious Royal Academy annual exhibition of 1866. The other event, at that stage unconnected with Tinworth but involving John Sparkes, concerned the pottery firm of Doulton & Co.

John Sparkes had, almost from the start of his association with Lambeth, believed that the way to give a practical purpose to the art training at his school was to forge links with local industry. The South London area surrounding his school was the centre for pottery manufacture and had been so for centuries. The industrial revolution had created demand for an immense range of clay products — many of a highly technical kind. The great building boom of the mid-century with its taste for highly elaborate surface decoration increasingly sought substitutes for stone carved ornamentation in the form of terra-cotta or other fired clay products such as Coade stone. The sanitary reforms initiated by Edwin Chadwick (who later sat for Tinworth) created a huge demand for pipe and sanitary fittings of all kinds. In nearly all these fields Doulton & Co. were the leaders. A complex series of mergers and family agreements in the 1850's had brought together several autonomous concerns with Henry Doulton, a younger son of John Doulton and the joint founder of Doulton & Watts, as the dominant partner.

It was therefore to Henry Doulton that John Sparkes came in 1859 with a proposition. Doulton & Co. had, in addition to their utilitarian wares, marketed a range of salt-glazed stoneware bottles of a more fanciful kind — mainly Toby Jugs and bottles formed as caricatures of politicians and other prominent people. In Germany over many centuries a magnificent tradition of elaborately decorated salt-glazed ornamental ware had flourished known as "Gres de Flandres". However, changing social circumstances and, in particular, the imposition of a salt tax had largely destroyed the industry. The proposition was to revive the art at Lambeth and in consequence provide employment for Sparkes' pupils.

At first the idea was received with indifference by Henry Doulton, whose energies were firmly committed to the more practical aspects of the company. However, over the next six years influence was brought to bear on him from a close friend, Edward Cresy, an engineering inspector associated with the ambitious sanitary undertakings which Doulton's serviced. A man of great perception and sensitivity, he had acquired from an artist acquaintance, Henry Stacy Marks, an old Rhenish salt-cellar. It was this elaborate object, incised with linear designs, embellished with decorated bosses and with cobalt blue slip colouring the cold grey clay body, which he used in an effort to wean Henry Doulton from his initial hostility.

As the pre-eminent position of Doulton & Co. became more secure and publicly acknowledged through their success at exhibitions, Henry Doulton turned more to artistic concerns. He read and admired John Ruskin and, with more leisure, began to travel extensively in Europe — enlarging his perception of the world of art in the process.

The 1862 International Exhibition in London was a triumph for Doulton with gold medals and commendations for their display; however, amongst the pipes and sanitary ware was an incongruous object — a clumsy copy of the Rhenish salt-cellar made at Cresy's behest which, perhaps fortunately, attracted little attention. In the meantime John Sparkes had established contacts with other potters, including William De Morgan. Again he approached Henry Doulton, this time with examples of his pupils' work. Circumstances were now different; he was warmly received and invited to dinner where he met Edward Cresy for the first time. Their combined influence set in train the Doulton Art Pottery enterprise which, by 1866, was ready to be launched — although it would be another seven years before John Sparkes, on a "wet and dismal morning",[1] led his band of pupils in a procession from Millers Lane to take over the specially prepared Art Pottery accommodation at Doulton's.

George Tinworth's family circumstances suffered a further blow in 1866 with the death of his father who had, according to George, become a reformed character in his last months. Tinworth now had to take over responsibility for the wheelwright's business and support his mother and younger brother from the proceeds. This waste of talent appalled Sparkes, who had admired the plaster group by Tinworth in that year's Academy. It was called "Peace and Wrath in Low Life" and was exhibited the following year in the 1867 Paris International Exhibition. Afterwards, the plaster was broken up and all that now remains is the description by Gosse, based on John Sparkes' memory of it: "The scene was taken from his own doors; it was a page from the gutter-life at Hope St., Walworth. Two little boys were fighting, two little girls were trying to separate them or egging them on, as the case might be. A dog in the foreground was barking with lively interest in the whole affair." Sparkes recognised the skill in portraying character and the primitive vigour breaking through the "timid conventionality" of the technique. He therefore persuaded Henry Doulton to offer Tinworth a job at Doulton & Co., paying him thirty shilling a week initially — which they had previously ascertained was approximately what he earned from the wheelwright business.

It is characteristic of Tinworth that, in recalling this event, he first notes in true old testament fashion that his fate had been prefigured in the treacle battle already recounted — for he had observed that one of his brothers in the scrimmage had sported a political slogan on his cap: "Doulton for Lambeth". His ambition was to become a professional sculptor and, as he laboured at the wheelwright's shop, his mind dwelt on his heartfelt wish: "The wish was like a prayer. A wish and a prayer are both the same."

For some time, however, the reality fell far short of his hopes: "I was told to be at the Pottery on Monday morning at seven o'clock. I got there before the gates opened and all the men and boys were standing outside waiting for the bell to ring . . . The men were bringing out one of their vans, and they said to me 'Now then, pretty feet, get out of the way'. I could put up with that for I had been knocked about in Walworth before I went to Lambeth." He had been told to report to the manager, Mr. Brion, and was surprised to find him involved in the practical work, with his shirt sleeves tucked up, putting slip into a plaster mould. No special provision had been made and Tinworth was put to work on touching up filters; he felt let down and unwanted: "I seemed to get no encouragement and I was in misery all that time."

But behind the scenes John Sparkes continued to support him. He persuaded Doulton's to shorten his working day to the surprisingly lenient hours of nine a.m. to five p.m., and he was set to work modelling huge medallions copied from ancient coins and executed in terra-cotta. One of these representing Hercules wearing a lions-head hood (fig. 5) was admired by

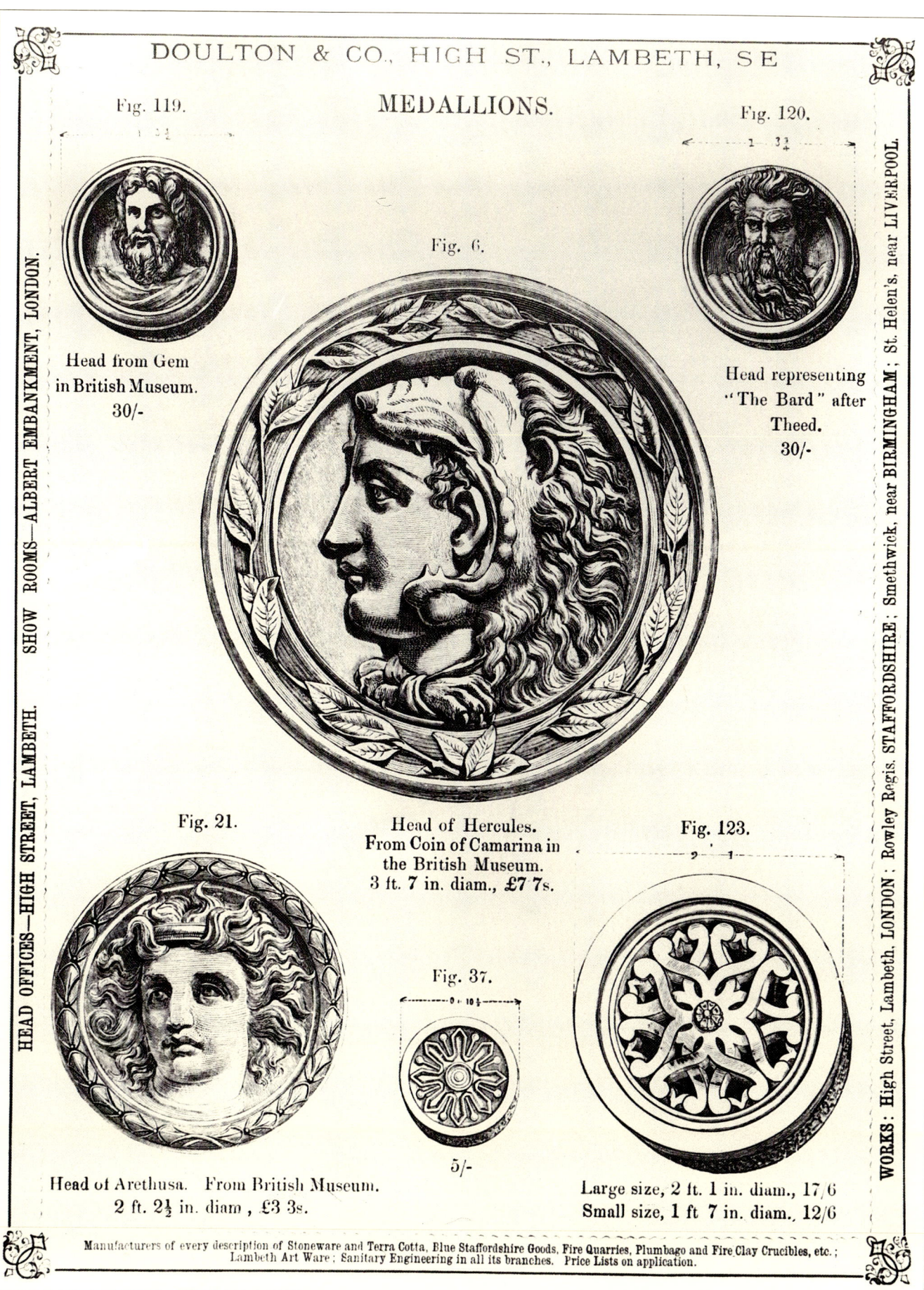

Fig. 5. A page from a Doulton & Co. catalogue illustrating medallions by George Tinworth.

John Ruskin, who, on the occasion of giving prizes at the Lambeth Schools, used it as his text for demonstrating the true principles of relief. A surprising choice, as Gosse notes, in the light of his later strictures on Tinworth's failure to observe those principles. Circumstances began to work in Tinworth's favour. The firm decided to develop their interest in terra-cotta and James Doulton, a cousin of Henry, was brought in to manage it.

At the same time, Tinworth began to decorate pottery which was exhibited for the first time in 1867 at the Paris exhibition and at Kensington. In 1868 he exhibited for a second time at the Academy. John Doulton, father of Henry, sat for a terra-cotta bust portrait by him. A working potter like his son, he was direct and down to earth: "I never see you sweat" he said to Tinworth, "when I was a young man the sweat used to run off my nose." The bust, according to Gosse, was "scarcely a work of merit." Fortunately, it passed the acid test of being a likeness, for, one lunch-time, the old man brought his granddaughter, Kitty, a child of fourteen or so, to see it. A game was played with her, the cloth covering the unfired clay model was whisked away: " 'Who is that my dear?' She said 'Why, you Grandpa.' Then he kissed her. It was an anxious moment for me." The following year Tinworth carried out a more ambitious work, a fountain designed by John Sparkes which, after being exhibited, was installed in Kennington Park.

Four years elapsed before any further piece was exhibited at the Academy. In the meantime much was happening at Doulton & Co. in developing the Art Pottery. Tinworth was given assistants, some of whom achieved distinction later as artists in their own right. Alongside him worked the Barlows, first Arthur, then Hannah and later Lucy and Florence; the younger brothers of Wallace Martin, Walter and briefly Edwin; Frank Butler, deaf and almost dumb and, after the establishment of the special studios in 1873, hundreds of others.

It must be assumed that Tinworth became increasingly aloof. He enjoyed a special status, partly because he predated all his new companions in the enterprise, but mainly as a consequence of a somewhat awe-struck recognition of the great talent in their midst. Tinworth's own work, therefore, follows an independent course — with the exception of his decorated pots. However, these too, in retaining a continuity of ideas and methods, are unrelated to the changing fashions pursued by the others at Doulton's. The fortunes of the art pottery at Lambeth have been described fully elsewhere, notably by Desmond Eyles[2], and therefore will be referred to only when relevant to Tinworth's own development.

Tinworth's earliest sculptural work at Doulton's was not in terra-cotta, but in salt glaze stoneware. It generally took the form of small panels, vigorously and deeply modelled in high relief, of biblical subjects such as "The Casting Out of the Money-Lenders" and "The Wise and the Foolish" — both in the Harriman-Judd Collection (Plates 65 & 66). Similar panels, twelve in all, were incorporated into an ebonised cabinet purchased by the Victoria & Albert Museum in 1872 (fig. 6). They relate closely to an elaborate salt-cellar made for Henry Doulton in 1871 which incorporates scenes from the last hours of the life of Christ on its four sides. The primitive vigour of these early pieces appeals strongly to modern taste which sets high store on originality and closeness to the inspirational source. Gosse thought otherwise: "These panels were executed very rudely, in the plain green clay with some rough admixture of blue, and look like quaint productions of some ingenious old German potter, struggling with a material which he had but poorly understood. It is amusing to compare these primitive conceptions of Biblical narrative with the artist's later treatment of the same scenes."

Tinworth's circumstances and status rapidly improved. In 1873, after the

Fig. 6. Cabinet 1871: designed by Charles Bevan with plaques by George Tinworth. (*Victoria and Albert Museum,* London)

end of the Franco-Prussian war, Henry Doulton proposed that Tinworth visit France and Belgium as companion to his cousin, James Doulton. Perhaps no other circumstance in the relationship between Tinworth and the Doulton family speaks so clearly of the closeness, absence of class prejudice, and freemasonry of talent underpinning the friendship. Each stage of the journey was a kaleidoscope of new experiences: "I never knew the sea could show all the colours of the rainbow." He was high spirited enough by the time they reached the river Seine to deliver an excrutiating pun to his travelling companions: "If I was to bathe in it I should be insane."

Paris, after a brief period of adjustment made more difficult by the still unrepaired devastation of the Commune and the Franco-Prussian war which preceded it, was much to his taste. He spent most of his time sketching vases in the Sevres Museum where he was treated with great kindness and, in spite of his lack of French, met and enjoyed the company of the officials, their families and friends. His sight-seeing included climbing to the top of the Arc de Triomphe, visiting Napoleon's tomb and, of course, the Louvre: "The French have got Venus de Milo in this place and of all people they deserve it for they know how to appreciate it and how to place it, which is more." His enthusiasm for Paris was boundless: "Why is it that to me sculpture seems more at home in Paris than it does in this country? I think it is because there is a greater mixture of Greek and Roman blood among the French than there is in the English. I often wish that I could have lived in Paris and learned things I wanted to know, but perhaps it is all for the best, people think I might not have been so original if I had."

On his return, the intimacy with the Doulton family continued with regular visits to their country estates. All concerned clearly enjoyed the unaffected relationship which must have been in striking contrast to the general practice of Victorian formality with its extreme respect for the niceties of social and class background.

The mid-seventies marked the beginning of Tinworth's period of greatest achievements. It was also for Doulton & Co. a time when their attention turned towards America. Following the success of the first International Exhibition in 1851, or to give it its full title, the "Great Exhibition of the Works of Industry of all Nations", similar displays of manufactured goods and the fine and applied arts were mounted every few years in Europe and America.

These trade fairs, as they would now be called, offered manufacturers a splendid opportunity for introducing their latest products on to a world market. Success depended upon the winning of medals and other citations awarded by panels of leading experts in the field, who pronounced on each class of goods in thorough and forthright terms which today would be scarcely imaginable. Manufacturers and customers laid great store by these judgements which undoubtedly played a considerable role in the commercial success of products. Much effort was put into creating a lavish setting for the display. Workmen devoted their finest skills to creating special exhibition pieces far beyond any possible practical application except as objects for museums — which frequently they became. Doulton & Co. were no exception. On the contrary, they led the pottery field in the extravagance and comprehensiveness of their displays.

The Philadelphia Centennial Exhibition of 1876 provided Henry Doulton with a superb opportunity of demonstrating the great talents now in his employment and, in particular, those of George Tinworth. In addition to many small works, four major pieces either entirely by or incorporating work by him were exhibited: a pulpit in red and buff terra-cotta with five figure groups; a font with eight salt glazed panels; a reproduction in terra-cotta of John Bell's marble group "America" from the Albert Memorial in Kensington Gardens; and a large and elaborate Jug encircled with small relief panels of scenes from the bible (fig. 7). Further details of these pieces will be found in the chronology of George Tinworth's works. The *Art Journal*[3], in the first of its detailed surveys of the exhibition, illustrated a group of the salt-glazed pottery describing them as "true Art works, often of the very highest order; so good indeed as to grace the cabinet of the connoisseur, while brought within the reach of art lovers of means comparatively limited."

Between 1874 and 1876 Tinworth exhibited at the Royal Academy a number of terra-cotta panels of biblical subjects which received considerable

Fig. 7. Jug: Philadelphia Exhibition 1876. (*Smithsonian Institution, Washington*).

critical attention, notably from John Ruskin in his *Academy Notes* of 1875. John Ruskin still held the premier position in art-scholarship and criticism which he had occupied for a quarter of a century. It was not until the law-suit of 1878, when Whistler sued him successfully for defamation of character and was awarded a derisory farthing damages, that his health and judgement were seriously impaired.

Ruskin's comments on Tinworth were much quoted during the sculptor's lifetime. Writing about "The Release of Barabbas" (fig. 8), of which the first terra-cotta sketch was included in a frame of three studies, he declared that Tinworth is "full of fire and zealous faculty, breaking his way through all conventionalism to such truth as it can conceive; able also to conceive far more than can rightly be expressed on this scale. And after all the labours of past art on the Life of Christ, here is an English workman fastening, with more decision than I can recollect in any of them, on the gist of the sin of the Jews, and their rulers, in the choice of Barabbas, and making the physical fact of contrast between the man released and the man condemned clearly visible."

Fig. 8. Terra-cotta panel: "The Release of Barabbas".

Ruskin, no revolutionary (unlike some of his associates), saw the mob preference for the criminal as a condemnation of popular government; Tinworth's vision was a "flash of . . . prophetic intelligence on the question of Universal Suffrage." There then followed a devastating criticism: "But how it happens that, after millions of money have been spent on the machinery of art education at Kensington, an ornamental designer of so high a faculty . . . should never in his life have found a human being able to explain to him the first principle of relief . . . I must leave it to the Kensington authorities to explain." Had Ruskin forgotten that only a few years previously he had used Tinworth's medallion of Hercules as an exemplar of the true principles of relief modelling?

John Sparkes, by now recognised as a leading educationalist, continued to proselytise — notably at the Society of Arts.[4] In 1874 and again in 1880 he read papers on the history of the revival of saltglaze ware and described the work of the leading artists involved in the enterprise. He laid particular stress on one aspect of Tinworth's work which is in danger of being overlooked in documenting the major exhibition pieces. The Harriman-Judd collection is especially rich in examples of Tinworth's pottery design and decoration from the earliest period of his career. Sparkes included in his lectures a lyrical account[5] of his method and decorative style: "He prefers the clay soft from the thrower's wheel, so soft as to be too tender to handle. His delight is a spiral band or ornamental ribbon, sometimes deeply interdigitated, or elaborately frilled. The ornament usually covers as much surface as the ground and creeps or flies over the surface in wild luxuriance; bosses belts or bands of plain or carved moulding keep this wild growth to its work, put it in its place, and subject it to its use. No two pots are alike, and, although he has done many thousands, all different, he will still produce them in endless variety out of the same materials." Later in the same passage he describes a large jug similar to the one exhibited at Philadelphia as "perhaps the finest piece of decorated stoneware that has ever been produced in the modern age."

In 1876 Tinworth exhibited four works at the Royal Academy, including a terra-cotta panel of "David with the head of Goliath". This time not only

THE YORK MINSTER PANEL

1. OUR SAVIOUR ON THE CROSS
2. GIVING STUPEFING STUFF TO ONE OF THE THIVES
3. PETER BEHIND THE TREE
4. THE MOTHER
5. JOHN
6. MARY MAGDELEN
7. CASTING LOTS FOR THE COAT
8. THE COAT
9. PARTING HIS GARMENTS AMONG THEM,

THESE VISITORS COME INTO MY ROOM WHEN MODELING THIS PANEL GEORGE ELLIOT AND AND MRS LEWIS AND SIR H COLE OF SOUTH KENSINGTON WITH SIR H DOULTON H COLE SET DOWN IN FRONT OF THIS PANEL AND SAID, IT IS NOT VERY ORIGNAL, NOT AN ORIGNAL SUBJECT, THEN G ELLIOT COME AND SPOKE TO ME, SHE HAD RATHER A PLAIN FACE BUT YOU FORGOT ALL ABOUT HER FACE WHEN YOU HAD BEEN IN HER COMPANY 5 MINUTES SHE WANTED TO SEE HOW I HAD TREATED THE RELEASE OF BARRABUS BUT I COULD NOT FIND THE SKETCH. SHE TOLD ME NOT TO VEX MY SELF AT THE MOMENT, MR G LEWIS WAS LOOKING AT A SKETCH OF MINE RAISING OF LAZARUS AND HE SAID I HAD GIVEN POWER TO ONE OF THE FIGURE, WHICH I COULD NOT GET FROM A MODEL, SIR HENRY SAID THAT GEORGE ELLIOT WAS THE SHAKESPERE AMONG WOMAN.

Fig. 9. The York Minster panel: a page from George Tinworth's autobiography.

Ruskin but also George Edmund Street, an eminent architect, admired the pieces. They both visited Tinworth at Lambeth many times, giving encouragement and advice. At that time Street was engaged in two major ecclesiastical commissions. The first was the building of a new reredos at York Minster. The original intention was to carve the reredos in wood but, after lengthy experiments with clay mixes, an acceptable terra-cotta was produced. Tinworth designed and executed an ambitious Crucifixion which, although installed as designed, was later to be painted over, thus negating the quality of the terra-cotta finish (fig. 9).

The second was the rebuilding and decoration of the interior of the Royal Military Chapel (Guards' Chapel) in Birdcage Walk, London. Tinworth was asked to design twenty-eight semi-circular panels which were to be placed above the newly installed mosaic in the Guards' Chapel (fig. 10). He carried out a series of experimental models in saltglaze terra-cotta, seventeen of which are in the Harriman-Judd collection (plates 69-85), in order to explore the problems set by the high positioning of the finished pieces and their semi-

Fig. 10. The Guards' Chapel Lunettes. Two panels illustrated in the 1883 catalogue.

circular shape. Gosse states: "in the lunettes of the Guards' Chapel we find that he has learnt a lesson in good taste", meaning that he had moved some way towards recognising the "refinements of bas-relief", although he had still to actually apply them. Eventually those refinements destroyed the very qualities which his critics so admired. The lunettes remained in situ until the second world war when they were almost completely destroyed by enemy bombing. Two survive in damaged form and one "The Sowing of Tares" which, for some reason, was never used in the chapel, is still complete.[6]

The Academy exhibition of 1877 contained a secular work called "The Football Scrimmage" and in the same year Tinworth carried out another non-religious work, "The Wheelwright's Shop", portraying the episode from his own childhood already described. The previous year he had produced a series of four small salt-glaze panels of boys representing "The Seasons". These were commissioned by Lord Ronald Gower who had visited Tinworth in his studio. Two versions survive, one is in the Harriman-Judd collection (plates 160A,B; 161A,B). At this stage in his career there is a clear trend towards exploring contemporary and non-religious themes, allowing full rein to his love for portraying children and, in particular, boys at work and play.

The sense of fun and intense involvement, indeed identification, with the world of children characterises much of Tinworth's most deeply felt work, even when the seriousness of the chosen theme might have precluded such frivolity. Gosse was dismissive of the Academy piece which he refers to as "a scrimmage with portrait figures, which I am not able to commend." Some idea of this group, of which no other record survives, may be gained from a study of boys at play, a large free-standing sculptural group which forms part of the background to the photograph of Tinworth taken in old age (frontispiece). The light-hearted pieces portraying children, mice, frogs and occasionally other creatures in amusing or bizarre situations became a recurrent preoccupation when he needed relaxation from the serious business of modelling the large scale, prestigious religious pieces. Unlike these major works, documentation of such groups is sparse and their dating uncertain. The Harriman-Judd collection is particularly rich in examples of the secular works of Tinworth which are more to the modern taste than the biblical subjects and which may well show his talent at its most fruitful level of achievement.

Contemporary accounts understandably chronicle the major exhibition pieces. The Paris International exhibition of 1878 was the setting for Tinworth's most eccentric treatment of a biblical theme: a fountain in salt-glaze stoneware two metres in diameter and over two metres high, which portrayed, on a rising spiral in a series of vivid tableaux, scriptural subjects connected with the use of water (fig. 11). A recent reconstruction of this ambitious work[7], which had for many years been thought lost, demonstrated the most ingenious use of ducts and hollows in order to produce real water at the appropriate places. Gosse is predictably rather dismissive of this exuberant piece: "This has proved the most popular of all his productions but belongs more properly to his work as a decorative potter than to his work as a sculptor." Its popularity appears to have been shared by the French; one critic commended its "truly magisterial qualities" and considered it the finest of the Doulton exhibits.[8]

Tinworth was by now firmly embarked on the pursuit of what soon proved to be his undoing in Academic terms. In 1878, 1880 and 1881 he exhibited large scale terra-cotta friezes of great technical virtuosity. In 1882 he submitted an even larger panel "Preparing for the Crucifixion" c.144" (366cm) wide x 62" (157.5cm) high, which the Academy rejected on the grounds of its size. Their attitude is understandable when the practical considerations are taken into account. The main galleries were reserved for paintings and sculpture was by tradition exhibited in the Vestibule. The shock to Tinworth and to Henry Doulton was considerable, for the panel was undoubtedly one of the artist's finest works — showing to perfection his formidable powers over the marshalling of numerous figures into an intricately articulated frieze.

The rejection of the panel virtually marked the end of Tinworth's association with the Academy, although he did exhibit twice more. However, the reverse also had good consequences: Henry Doulton decided that a special exhibition of George Tinworth's major works should be held and that Edmund Gosse would be commissioned to write a catalogue introduction to a major publication on the sculptor.

The exhibition in Conduit Street in 1883 was an immediate and critically acclaimed success. It contained not only "Preparing for the Crucifixion" but also an equally large version of "The Release of Barabbas", the smaller version of which John Ruskin had written about so enthusiastically. "We had an exhibition of my work in Conduit Street, Regent Street, which turned out a success. The Prince and Princess of Wales opened it. Mr. Doulton gave me £20 out of it and the income-tax people took £17 out of it so I got £3 for

Fig. 11. Fountain. Paris Exhibition 1878.

myself. It is a hard nut to crack that a man gets up from the greatest poverty and by his talent and industry enriches his country and then the Government steps in and takes from him part of that which he has honestly earned." Edmund Gosse is more lyrical in his account:[9] "The Prince and the Princess of Wales came first, to a private view of their own, and the Princess was so much entertained and fascinated by the endless succession of animated scripture scenes that she was scarcely to be torn away to other social duties. She passed to her carriage at length, protesting against having to go so soon, with the vellum volume in her hands. Then a selected public came, and took an almost childish pleasure in the groups of gesticulating figures. Society accepted the occasion as a kind of glorified Sunday school class — piety and fine art combined. Then the general public and the thing became a furore. Again and again, after the stated period of the exhibition was over, Henry Doulton was wheedled into letting the show remain open a few days longer."

The vellum volume which Gosse observed clutched in the Princess of Wales's hands was his own splendidly produced commemorative work. It contains an introductory account of Tinworth's life and a critical appraisal of his work, a catalogue of works modelled by the sculptor and a series of finely produced photogravure illustrations of principal works. Gosse considered it with justification "a triumph of book production." Apart from this magnificent tribute to the sculptor, serious professional appraisal, although not uncritical, broadly accorded with general popular approval. J.A. Blaikie, in an extensive notice[10], described the exhibited works as a "revelation". "There can be no question that Mr. Tinworth is an artist of remarkable individuality. To such an extent is this the case that he stands quite alone, apart from his fellows, companionless." The *Illustrated London News* went further: "George Tinworth (is) now probably the most original, certainly the most independent artist in England" and the *Architect* considered "It is indeed a rare spectacle to see a manifestation of artistic energy so distinctly and vigorously individual." *The People* forecast that he "Bids fair to leave behind him works which will stamp him in his own life as one of the greatest artists of the world."

Chapter Three

1884-1897 Achievement and Maturity

With the success of the Conduit Street exhibition behind him, Tinworth, now aged forty and in artistic terms still a young man, continued to consolidate his reputation with major works. As Blaikie in the *Art Journal* review suggested: "The fields of Art are vast and varied; having accomplished much in Biblical illustration, he may do other and yet higher work in pastures new." These new fields were more difficult to explore than Blaikie supposed; at the same time a certain sameness and loss of vitality in new treatment of familiar subjects was becoming apparent.

A degree of tiredness and lack of originality was observed in the Doulton studios generally. In *Studio Notes No. 3*, dated April 1884[1], Mark V. Marshall, a highly talented artist recruited from the Martin Brothers, contributes a poetic "Lament".

> *"Oh Doulton ware, sweet Doulton ware,*
> *How varied all thy charms once were,*
> *With youthful vigor bold and free,*
> *How simple chaste you used to be.*
>   *Young Doulton Ware.*
> *Like Greek athlete stout Doulton ware,*
> *With "Gres-de-Flandre" for thy sire,*
> *Thy manhood's prime felt Tinworth's fire,*
> *It seemed thy strength would never tire.*
>   *Oh Doulton Ware.*
> *Dear Doulton Ware, Oh have a care,*
> *Thou art grown up in luxury*
> *And Roman splendours garnish thee*
> *Thy bounteous wealth drags heavily.*
>   *Oh Doulton Ware."*

This highly revealing warning cry continues for three more verses echoing a view which still persists amongst some present-day collectors of Doulton ware.

Despite Mark Marshall's doubts about the artistic quality of the products, his view found little public support and the eighties was a period of triumphant achievement for Doulton's. Exhibitions became almost annual events. At each one the Doulton stand was a major feature. John Sparkes designed a "highly ingenious and spacious pavilion with an Indian dome"[2] in glazed ceramic for the International Health Exhibition in 1884. Henry Doulton, "The Big Potter" as William De Morgan dubbed him, entertained the Prince and Princess of Wales in it. Similar pavilions were constructed for the Manchester Jubilee Exhibition of 1887 and the Glasgow International Exhibition of 1888. The whole range of Doulton products were put on display, but it was the art pottery which caught the public eye and attracted critical commendation. From a strictly commercial viewpoint, however, these products were not profitable: "Some parts of his business were not lucrative; the art work, for instance, never paid its way".[3] It has been estimated that Tinworth's Studio alone often involved a loss of over £1000 a year.[4] Some indication of the cost of purchasing a major panel by Tinworth is given in Mrs. Tinworth's diary for 1888 where she refers to "the unexpected success of a large panel which was sold for 500 guineas in 1880".[5]

A direct outcome of Edmund Gosse's championship of Tinworth was an ambitious terra-cotta panel based on a poem by the writer. A letter to Gosse dated July 12th, 1883 begins: "I am very glad to hear that you are pleased with the sketch that I made from your very clever poem. While reading it, the thought struck me that the Sons of Cydippe would make a very good panel . . . I should like to make a good panel of it to repay you for the honour that you have done me." The striking feature of the panel, a version of which is in the Harriman-Judd collection (plate 58), is that it is carried out in bas-relief with the more distant figures receding into almost ghostly obscurity. A paler cream-coloured slip has been used to assist the clarity of the composition and to suggest, although not consistently, local colour. The effect of this radical change so long advocated by Ruskin is to drain the composition of much of its vitality, substituting in its place a more conventional but academically respectable style.

Edmund Gosse's response to such a sensitive and ambitious gesture is unrecorded. Tinworth continued to write to him intermittently, sometimes seeking his support in submitting work to exhibitions, such as those at the Grosvenor Gallery. That Gallery exhibited a terra-cotta "Moses" in 1884 and "Genesis" in 1886, but later in the decade, according to Tinworth's wife, they rejected further contributions. Somewhat after this time he wrote again to Gosse offering a poem he had composed. "I want to know whether these lines are any good which came into my mind:

> *I thought I saw a happy pair,*
> *For the bridal day prepare,*
> *And then it passed away.*
> *Again another scene appears*
> *And all was turned to grief and tears*
> *For one is dead.*
> *Again I saw another sight,*
> *Among the redeemed was one in white,*
> *Sitting on a firmer throne,*
> *With a better robe and a brighter crown,*
> *That shall not pass away."*

Gosse's comments are unrecorded. We can guess that he would have reacted to this uneducated effort in the same dismissive way he had done to Tinworth's early and more vigorous sculpture.

The next few years marked a period of considerable success for Tinworth, with important commissions each year. The chronology of major works gives details of these. His last exhibited work at the Royal Academy was a bust of Sir Edwin Chadwick, the friend of Henry Doulton mentioned earlier, whose sanitary reforms had done so much for the health of London. He was an old man of eighty-five years by the time he sat for his portrait in 1886. Tinworth greatly admired him and considered he had "a fine well-balanced brain". Sir Edwin was notorious for the high opinion he held of himself: "He said he should like me to make his eyes in the bust the same as I had made the Saviour's eyes, with a benevolent look. I said to him, 'Do you think you are like Him?' He said, 'Well, I have saved thousands of lives', and by all accounts he had at the time of the cholera." He laid claim to having invented a number of revolutionary reforms: "He also told me he gave the idea for pictures to be placed in newspapers. Also the idea for the Police, although Peel got the credit for it." Tinworth was more charitable about Chadwick than Gosse, who described him as "this able, but grotesque and absurd being".[6]

The year 1888 is of special significance in developing our understanding of Tinworth's personal life. His wife Alice, thirteen years his junior, whom he had married on February 8th, 1881[7], kept a diary of her husband's professional and personal activities in that year, which has survived (fig. 12)[8]. Alice Tinworth (Digweed was her maiden name) was the daughter of a labourer. It is evident from the diary that there was a close, loving relationship although they had no children. It can be deduced from the domestic arrangements at the time of George Tinworth's death that ill-health incapacitated her at a relatively early age and that her sister had joined them in their house in Kew to look after them both. Somewhat surprisingly, George makes no mention whatsoever of his marriage in his autobiography.

By the start of the year 1888, it was becoming clear to them both that, in spite of George's celebrity, his work was not selling well. On Friday, 3rd February, Alice writes: "George often feels dreadfully discouraged, his panels not selling directly after he finishes them. He often says what a difference with him and painters. When a noted man paints a picture it is sold directly, but God orders all for the best and we must wait His own good time."

The somewhat envious reference to painting was very appropriate, for George had recently taken up painting and, during the course of the year,

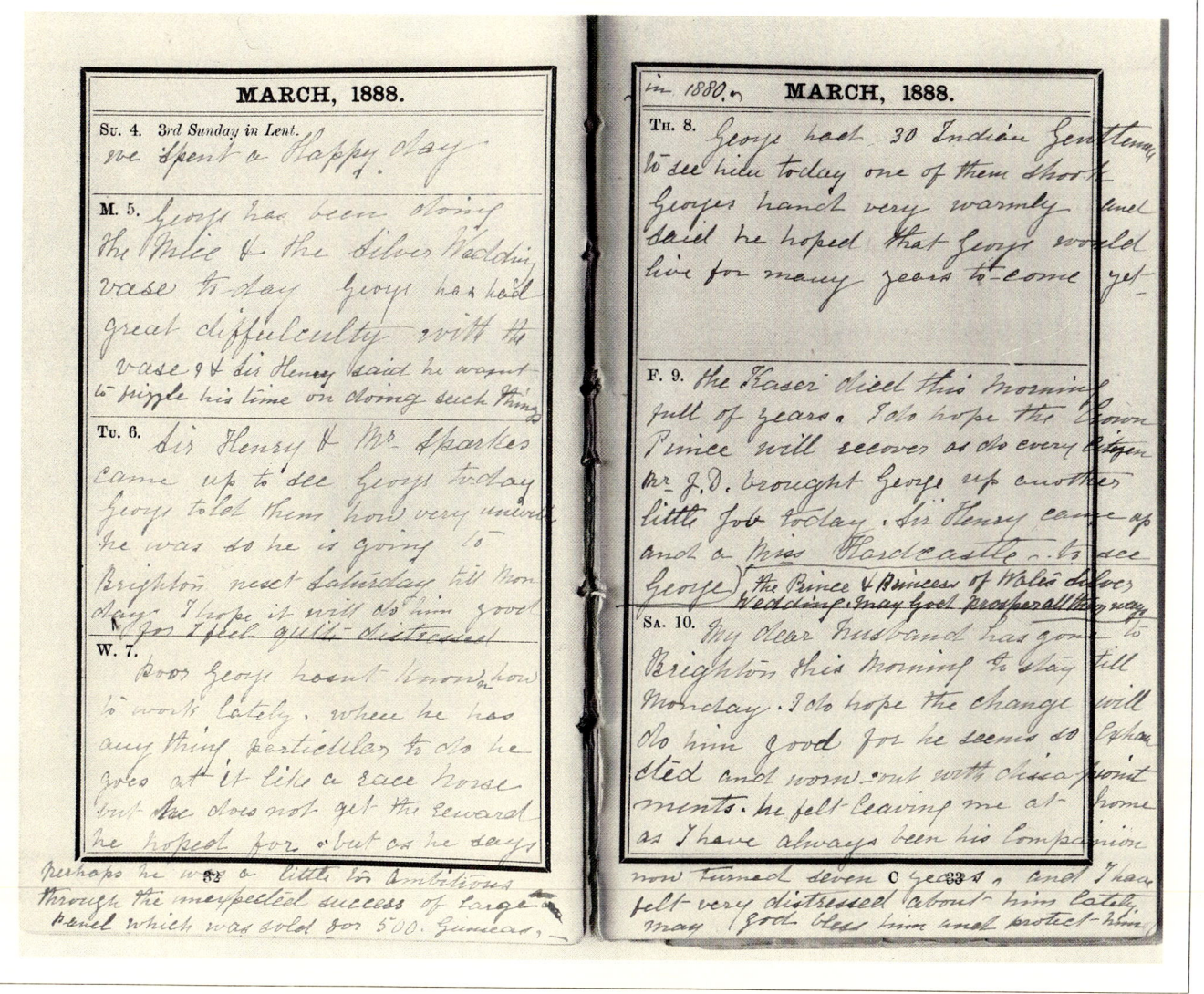

Fig. 12. Mrs. Tinworth's diary. March 4-March 10, 1888.

completed several portraits of his wife in water-colours and oils. These were proudly taken to the local picture framers by Alice: "I took my portrait in oil to be framed this morning. The man said he could see it was done by someone who loved Art and a great improvement from the last one." Tinworth's motives in pursuing this new line are made clear: "George paints a little every evening and he is getting on very nicely. I am so glad for him, dear old boy, it will make him to feel a little more independent".

The frequent bouts of depression were undermining Tinworth's health and on several occasions during the year he went to stay in Brighton for a few days. On his first visit he went alone and on Saturday the 10th of March Alice writes: "The Prince and Princess of Wales' Silver Wedding. May God prosper all their ways. My dear husband had gone to Brighton this morning. I do hope the change will do him good for he seems so exhausted and worn out with disappointments. He felt sad leaving me at home as I have always been his companion now turned seven years, and I have felt very distressed about him lately. May God bless him and protect him". On Monday: "George returned from Brighton at half past six this morning; earlier than I expected. He was pleased to get home again and I feel much relieved that he feels better poor darling. He was so sadly before going away".

At the start of the year Tinworth was completing the Shaftesbury memorial panel which consisted of a relief portrait with three panels set underneath (fig. 13). Troubles over breakages during firing beset him and contributed to his depression. By present-day standards, however, Tinworth was engaged in an impressive variety of work. A number of new frog and mouse groups were created and it appears that he could happily put down his tools one day, after working on a religious panel, and immediately and without incongruity, embark on a highly frivolous piece of animal sculpture. These humorous pieces were much appreciated; Alice notes that "out of forty different mice that George has designed they want two of each for the Showroom".

On Friday, 17th February, Sir Henry Doulton, who had been knighted by Queen Victoria at Osborne the previous August, gave a lecture at the Royal Institute: "George took me to the Royal Institute this evening to hear Sir Henry Doulton on Pottery. It turned out a great success. We were both very pleased. There was a fine audience and the carriages reached as far as Piccadilly. The library looked very nice with Art Pottery artistically arranged. Sir Henry spoke up about George well, and there was ten of his Panels shown by the Magic Lantern. They were beyond my expectations". The following Wednesday Sir Henry called on George in his studio and "told him how far the carriages reached and what a fine audience at the Institute. George said he might have said he knew they did as we found our carriage in Piccadilly, a penny bus!"

Throughout the year Sir Henry's visits to Tinworth are noted, as are the numerous other visitors of all ages and types. On the 24th of July: "Seven old ladies mounted up the stairs to see George. Their ages were five over seventy and two over eighty years. They were so pleased to see him and when they left they said God bless you with the blessing that maketh rich and addeth no sorrow thereto."

On the night of Wednesday, 12th December, disaster struck the pottery firm. A fire destroyed the main part of the pottery. The first indication George Tinworth had was a bill-poster on the station platform on his way to work: "He was so terrified when he saw the bills at the station he never had a more miserable ride in his life because he didn't know which part was burnt. When he arrived he discovered that many of his moulds had been destroyed in the flames. The fire was extremely large and destructive. "It ranked as the biggest London fire of the year" according to Gosse.[9] For Sir Henry it was the second catastrophe in a few weeks; his wife died at the end of October after a long illness. Like Tinworth, he first heard of the fire on his way to the works the following morning: "He seemed stunned, bewildered, and as he gazed on the charred ruins, the tears ran down his cheeks."[10] His breakdown lasted only a few moments and characteristically, seeing the groups of dejected workmen standing about, their livelihood gone, he said to his managers: "Well, now what are we going to do? You must employ all these men, mind – all of them!"

Tinworth's own studio was apparently undamaged and the following Monday he was buying photographs of the ruins of the pottery works.

Immediately after Christmas he received an order to carry out a large panel to commemorate the life of Samuel Morley, the distinguished educationalist, for the newly built Morley College (fig. 14). This lunette in both size and shape

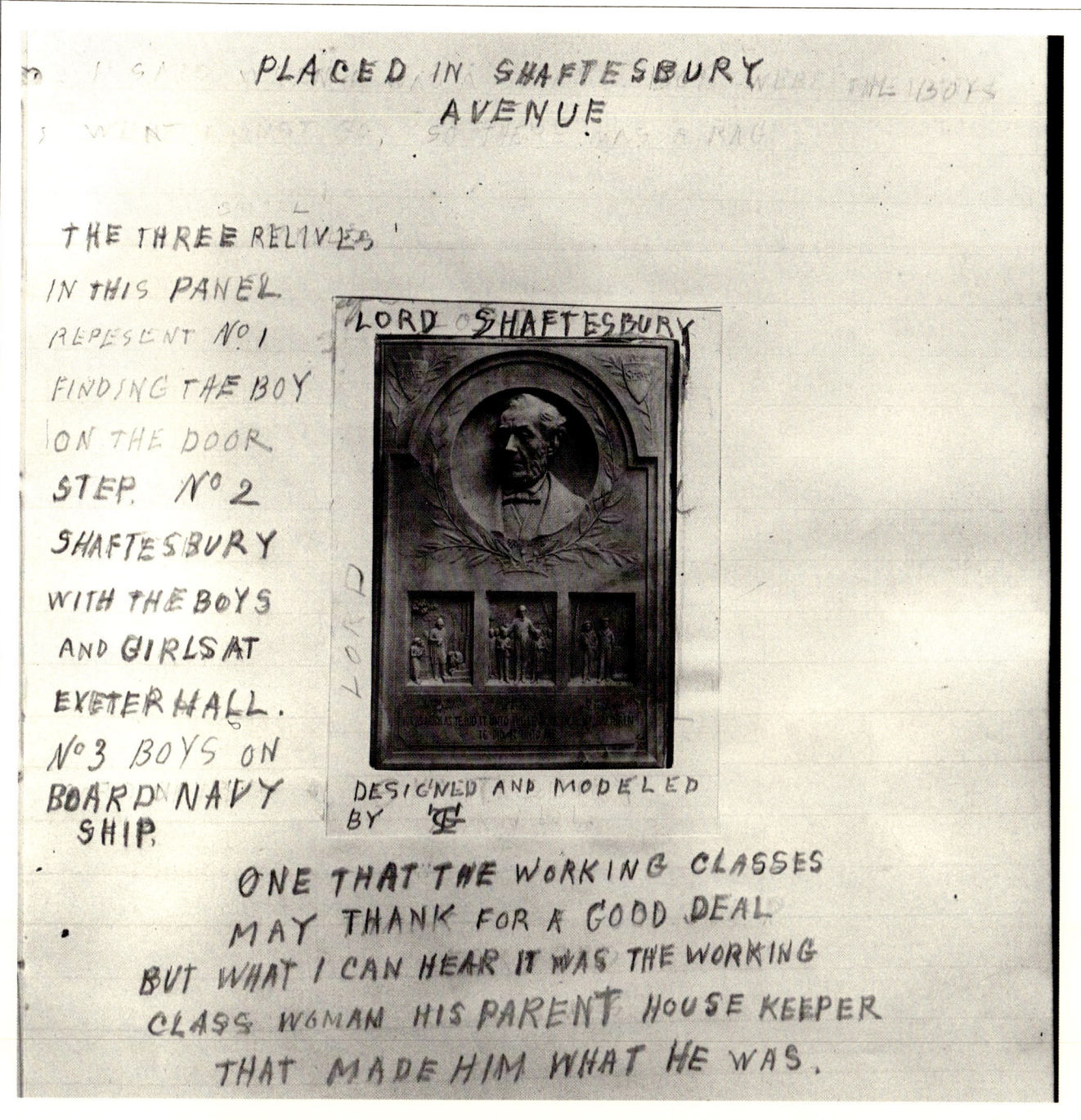

Fig. 13. The Shaftesbury Memorial: a page from George Tinworth's autobiography.

resembled the over-door panel which Tinworth had modelled for the new Doulton Art Pottery headquarters in Lambeth and, similarly, it was designed to go over the entrance. Both the pieces contain contemporary portraits and demonstrate how rewarding a greater concentration on sculpture based on modern, non-religious subjects would have been. John Sparkes chose the Samuel Morley lunette as the first mast-head illustration in his manual *"Potters: Their Arts & Crafts."*

The next few years continued the pattern revealed in Alice Tinworth's diary. Major commissions were rare in spite of discreet advertising by Doulton & Co. An 1890 pamphlet issued by the firm entitled "Sculpture in Terra Cotta by George Tinworth" contained selected critical comments, lists of illustrations which had appeared in journals, the title and location of major works, and finally a statement to customers that: "Architects and others who

Fig. 14. Terra-cotta panel. Morley College, 1889.

are contemplating the use of terra-cotta Sculpture can obtain further particulars of Mr. Tinworth's works from: — Messrs Doulton & Co."

The largest memorial work designed and executed by Tinworth was the monument to Professor Henry Fawcett MA, erected in Vauxhall Park in 1893. The height was about sixteen feet. The monument consisted of a pedestal, with eight relief panels set into it, surmounted by a larger than life-size seated figure of the blind MP, who was a Member of four Parliaments and, from 1880 to 1884, was Postmaster General. Standing behind him was the figure of Victory holding a wreath over his head (fig. 15). The group was financed and later presented to the Park by Sir Henry Doulton and was therefore not a public commission.

Another major work carried out during the early 1890's was an internal commission also. It was designed for exhibition at the Chicago World Fair of 1893 and took the form of a huge vase standing over fifty inches high. The "History of England" vase, as it was called, is now in the Harriman-Judd collection and details of it will be found in the catalogue (plates 52-55). The salt-glaze groups depicting scenes from English history are particularly lively and recall the primitive salt-glaze panels of the early 1870s; it also resembles the large jug exhibited at the Philadelphia Centennial Exhibition in 1876. Unlike the earlier piece, however, it does not appear to have attracted any contemporary critical mention.

The following year, 1894, a memorial group to the famous non-conformist preacher, the Reverend Charles Hadden Spurgeon, was commissioned. Spurgeon had visited Tinworth in his studio years before when he was modelling the Guards' Chapel Lunettes and had provided him with the esoteric biblical information "that Satan always sowed with his left hand." Tinworth admired him greatly and perhaps in consequence designed a strikingly original and effective memorial which was erected at the Spurgeon Orphanage, Stockwell, London (fig. 16).

Sir Henry Doulton continued to champion the cause of the Art Pottery and to guard the interests and well-being of his workers, although he dealt ruthlessly with a group of strikers who he considered had acted selfishly and disloyally. In May of 1896 Sir Henry became seriously ill. Gosse describes the event very movingly: "Just, however, as the spring was breaking with peculiar loveliness upon all the sweeps and dingles of his Surrey home, he had a warning so serious that it took the sunshine out of his life."[11] Over the next eighteen months his health deteriorated steadily and he suffered great pain. He died on the 17th of November, 1897 (fig. 17).

Fig. 15. George Tinworth working on the model of the Fawcett Monument, 1892-93.

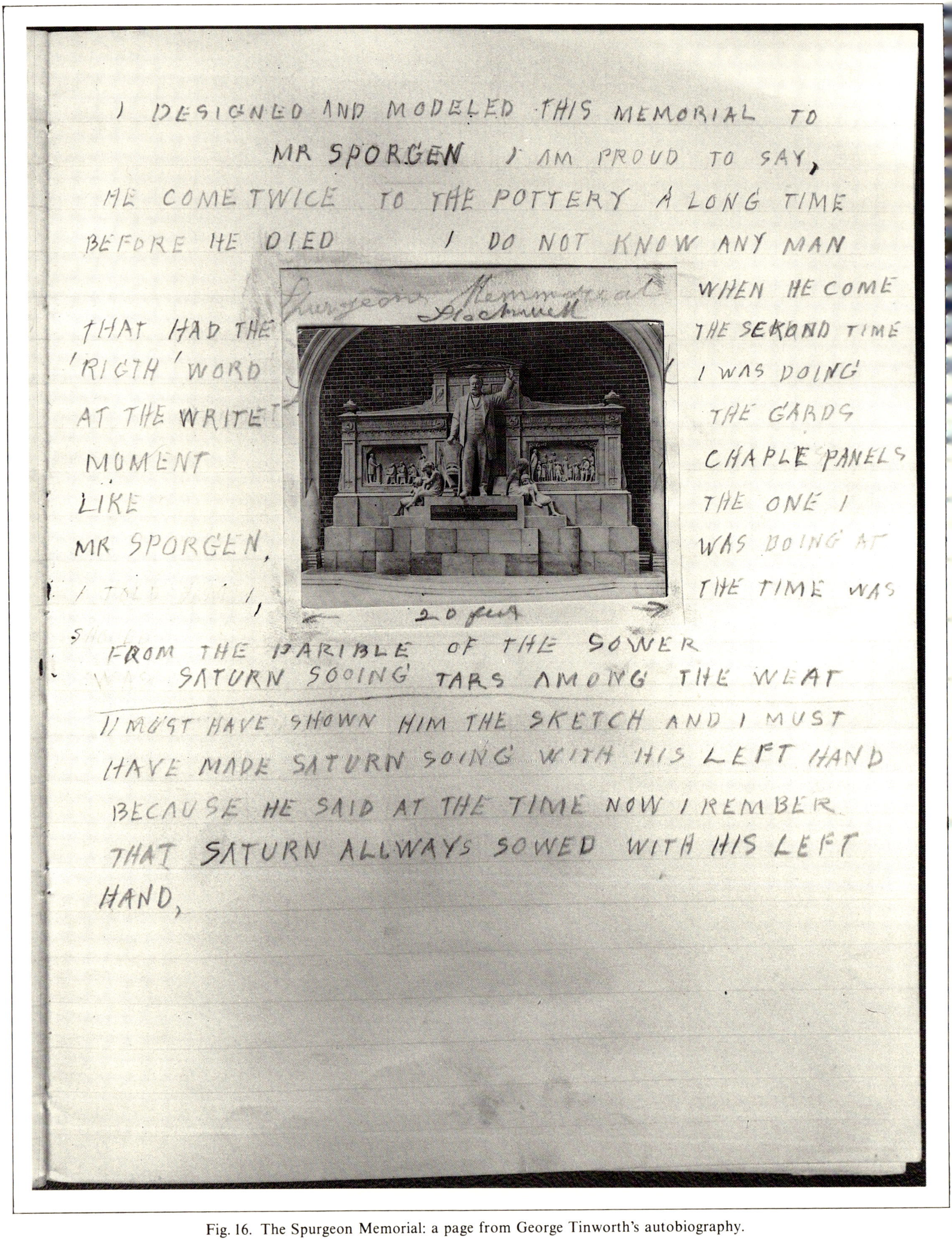

I DESIGNED AND MODELED THIS MEMORIAL TO
MR SPORGEN I AM PROUD TO SAY,
HE COME TWICE TO THE POTTERY A LONG TIME
BEFORE HE DIED   I DO NOT KNOW ANY MAN
WHEN HE COME
THAT HAD THE   THE SEKOND TIME
'RIGTH' WORD   I WAS DOING
AT THE WRITE   THE GARDS
MOMENT   CHAPLE PANELS
LIKE   THE ONE I
MR SPORGEN,   WAS DOING AT
                                                THE TIME WAS
FROM THE PARIBLE OF THE SOWER
SATURN SOOING TARS AMONG THE WEAT
I MUST HAVE SHOWN HIM THE SKETCH AND I MUST
HAVE MADE SATURN SOING WITH HIS LEFT HAND
BECAUSE HE SAID AT THE TIME NOW I REMBER
THAT SATURN ALLWAYS SOWED WITH HIS LEFT
HAND,

Fig. 16. The Spurgeon Memorial: a page from George Tinworth's autobiography.

SIR H DOULTON AS TOLD US AFTER STICKING TO BUSINESS FOR YEARS IN HIS YOUNG DAYS, HE WAS INVITED DOWN INTO THE COUNTRY AND THE TRAIN GOT TO THE STATION, BEFORE HIS FRIENDS GOT THERE TO MEET HIM, THEN HE SAID TO HIMSELF WHAT HAVE I BEEN DOING ALL THIS TIME, AND NOT HAVE SPENT SOME TIME NOW AND THEN DOWN HERE IN THIS BEAUTIFUL COUNTRY BEFORE. I should think it must have been a beautiful day in the spring time;

SIR HENRY WAS A GREAT LOVER OF ART, AND GAVE INCOURAGEMENT TO ME, MANY A TIME,

WHEN PASSMORE EDWARDS STOOD UP TO ME A LITTLE WHILE FOR HIS PORTRAITE, I SAID IF THERE WAS NO ART OR MUSIC WE MIGHT AS WELL LIVE ON CARROTS AND TURNIPS. AND HIS ANSWER WAS, THATS WHAT IT IS COMEING TO.

HE TOLD ME IF HE HAD TO GO THROUGH THE TROUBLE HE HAD WITH HIS PIPE WORKS DOWN THE COUNTRY HE WOULD SOONER GO ON THE WHEEL AGAIN. I THINK IT WAS THE MACHINERY KEPT GETING OUT OF ORDER, THIS WAS BEFORE I COME I SHOULD THINK

Fig. 17. Sir Henry Doulton: a page from George Tinworth's autobiography.

Chapter Four

1898-1913 Decline and Final Years

The death of Sir Henry Doulton in 1897 marked the end of the most intensive and productive period in Tinworth's career. Although a further sixteen years lay ahead, with continuing recognition of his specially favoured status within the firm, public demand for his work flagged, particularly for his large terra-cotta religious pieces.

Sir Henry Doulton's continuous and enthusiastic championship of Tinworth was only part of the strikingly enlightened relationship he had cultivated with the work force at Doulton's. By present-day standards he would be judged insufferably paternalistic, yet his deeply caring concern for the welfare of his employees embraced attitudes which even today are rare.

George Tinworth, who must have been amongst the 1500 of his employees attending the funeral at West Norwood on Monday, the 22nd of November, suffered what he describes as a nervous breakdown: "I used to sit before my work and my arms would drop at my side and, although I wanted to work, I could not." His response to this state of depression was extraordinarily enterprising; he booked a Cooks' tour to Rome at a cost of about £17. He adopted an independent attitude to the arrangements, travelling out a day in advance of the main party, meeting them in Paris. The train journey to Rome was marked by a farcical episode during the overnight stay at a hotel in Genoa: "When I got into the room a tom cat came out. On the centre of the bed lay two mice close together like 'Babes in the Wood' — the room was well scented!" Fortunately it turned out that the next room was intended for him: "I was very glad, I did not care for mice or cats in my bedroom."

For George Tinworth, Rome was a religious rather than a visual or artistic experience: St. Peter's, the symbolic fulfillment of a biblical prophecy, rather than a witness to the overwhelming greatness of his illustrious sculptor predecessor Michaelangelo. The Catacombs raised in his mind the thought: "How the poor Christians could live down there in the catacombs I do not know." Yet the immediacy of the past was for him a direct, unaffected experience. Commenting on a visit to the Pantheon, which he notes was restored by Hadrian, whom he describes as "the General that used to walk about England with his soldiers bare-headed", he makes a tart swipe at Roman weather (it had been raining continuously for three weeks): "If it could rain for three weeks right off in Rome in Hadrian's time no wonder he believed in public baths, to have a good sweat."

The persistent rain gave him a cold and with characteristic determination he insisted on a Roman chemist making up his favourite remedy of sage and vinegar. He also decided to start the return journey in advance of his companions, stopping off at Pisa, Genoa, Turin and Aix-les-Bains before arriving back at Paris. It was on this occasion that he discovered the exclusion of his name from the members of the French Academy described earlier.

He returned to England via Dover, still carrying his bottle of sage and vinegar. Fortunately his recovery from the cold and, more importantly from his depression, was complete and he was immediately back at work on the panel "Paul Entering into Rome".

Between 1895 and 1897 the Reverend R.E. Walsh MA visited George Tinworth's studio at least twice. He recorded his impressions in articles published in *The Young Woman* and in the *Sunday Magazine*[1]. "Our great Artist in Terra-Cotta is 'like a star, and dwells apart.' To find him you must mount well nigh to star land — at least to the pinnacle of the Messrs. Doultons' lofty pile of buildings that figure so prominently in the striking view to be obtained from Westminster Bridge. To the big thronging world that en passant sees only curious photographs of his Scripture panels in shop-windows, he is a strange, remote genius. He does not appear among fashionable groups in art circles. Here in his high retreat in the great Lambeth Pottery, retained and consulted by the Doultons, this unique and original potter-sculptor quietly and freely works out his own peculiar vein of art in his own guileless way." Having mounted those numerous stairs fired by his somewhat over-wrought romanticism, the Reverend Walsh discovered the surroundings of the sculptor's studio "unpoetic" with the vague shapes of huge pieces of work shrouded in damp cloths, including rather mysteriously "a sturdy English model half hid in a recess of the studio." The mice which had been "favoured frequenters" of the studio (and even been given names) had latterly overstayed their welcome. Having made "mincemeat" of Tinworth's clothes, they had to be trapped. Tinworth himself was wearing a "thin linen workmanlike coat", shaking his hand with the same direct and unaffected pleasure which he showed to all his visitors, be they Princes, statesmen, bishops, critics, the eminent or the merely curious.

The Reverend Walsh was shown the numerous terra-cotta works languishing under their wraps, many of them presumably unfired: "The Judgement of Solomon", "Agony in Gethsemane", "Christ before Herod" and a somewhat "delapidated design in the rough", "Noah Constructing his Ark", which on a later visit had been worked on again. On that later visit he mentions a series based upon Moses and the Exodus and a commission for Shelton Parish Church of a Crucifixion.

Throughout both of the articles written by the Reverend Walsh there is a clear perception of the particular qualities Tinworth brought to his portrayals of biblical scenes: "Not only is there nothing conventional about him — neither classic nor Italian, but he brings with him a South London workman's ideas of real life, of human figures, sturdy and sometimes rather studied (he models from the life), of lively street scenes with byplay among the gamins, such as may be seen in the Lambeth street named after him . . . ". "It is the Bible as the lower middle-class Evangelicals see it . . . He is a Puritan — and very rarely presents the nude (for example, in scenes from Eden). At the same time he has the flavour and mother-wit of 'pawky' humorists like Bunyan, Quarles and Andrew Fuller."

In the later article this view of Tinworth was further developed: "Mr. Tinworth strikes you as homely, single-hearted, plain and direct of speech, endowed with a 'pawky' humour that plays in glints about his eyes. There is a fine natural independence about this workman-artist. He is every whit his sturdy, genial, natural self, not less so in the presence of the Princess of Wales and Mr. Ruskin." He concludes that "a course in Tinworth is a liberal education in Christian Truth."

In June 1902, the *Pottery Gazette* published an interview with Tinworth in which he described his method of work in some detail: "Sometimes I make sketches on paper and sometimes sketches in clay but then again I sometimes work without sketches. Here is a small clay sketch of that panel there: 'The Wise Men Opening Their Treasures'. You see I have altered these figures in the composition itself. But when I sketched my 'Release of Barabbas' in clay I never moved a figure afterwards. I often think of my work at night as I go to sleep, and have done so for thirty years, and it is with me when I wake."

According to Walter Fairhall[2], in 1902 Tinworth was working on a series of panels illustrating the events leading to the Crucifixion of Christ. There were fourteen of these which were reproduced from moulds by his assistant, William Hollowell. The vertical format of these panels created compositional difficulties which Tinworth was ill equipped to solve. An exception to this is panel XIII illustrating Jesus being taken down from the cross and entitled "All Misery Past" (fig. 19), a subject already dealt with several times. In this panel the grid-like framework of ladders against the cross is counterpointed by strong diagonals of arms and struts, forming a powerful and striking composition.

A small booklet about the panels, called "From Sunset to Sunset", was

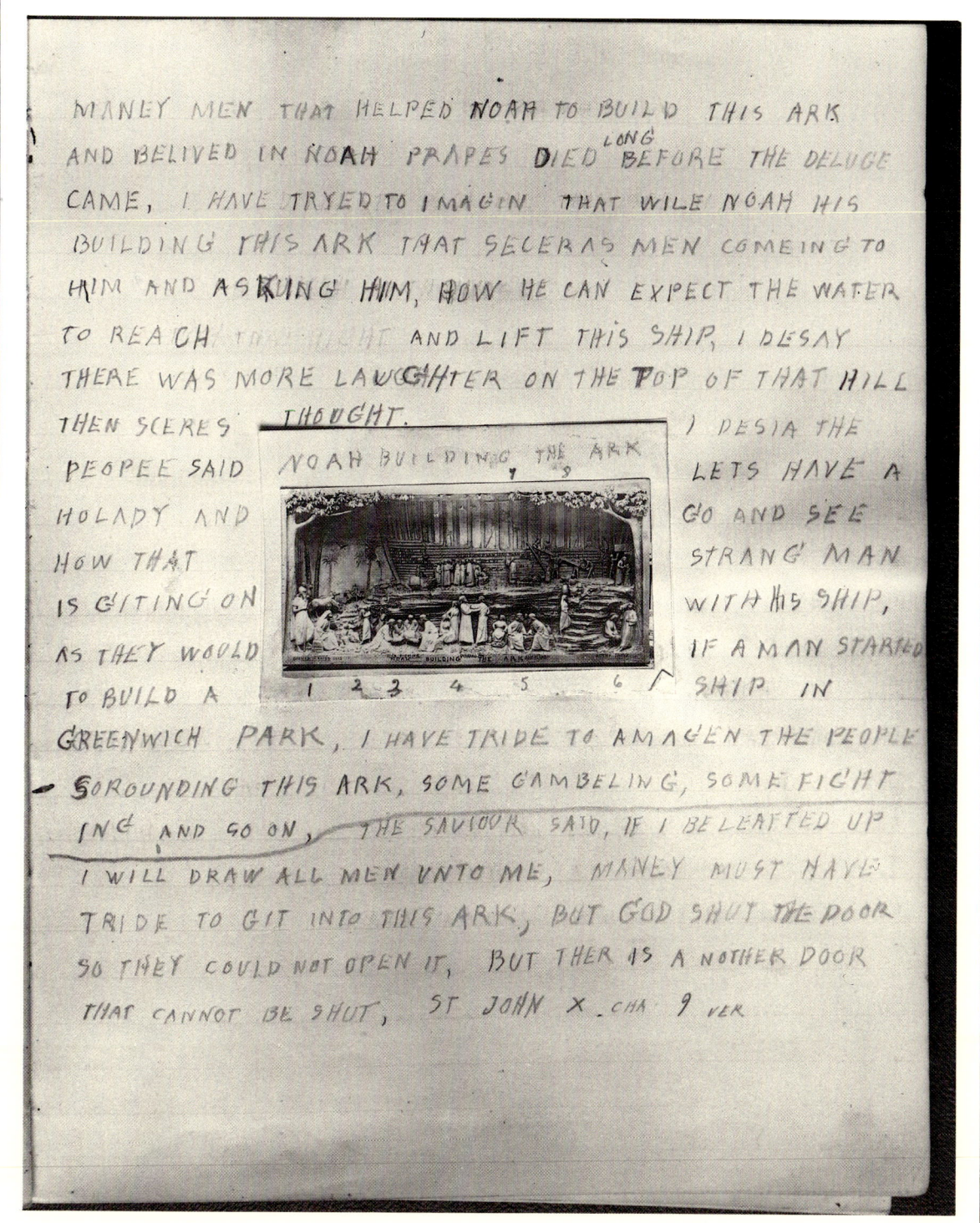

Fig. 18. *"Noah Constructing his Ark"*: a page from George Tinworth's autobiography.

Fig. 19. Terra-cotta panel: *"All Misery Past"*.

issued by Doulton's and went through at least two editions. All fourteen panels were illustrated by photographs and accompanied by texts compiled by Tinworth. A discrete advertisement at the back of the second edition of the booklet reveals that the panels are from the "collection" of Messrs. Doulton & Co. Ltd. "from whom further particulars can be obtained."[3] The gentle tenor of the language demonstrates again how far Doulton's were from any breath of brash commercialism. Unfortunately, sales of the terra-cotta panels were disappointing, possibly reflecting the somewhat stereotyped and flattened character of several of the panels.

An Australian, John Shorter Senior[4], an enthusiastic collector of Doulton Ware, knew both Tinworth and Henry Doulton, visiting the former in his studio. It was on one such occasion that the jocular point was made that brown (i.e. clay coloured) boy musicians would attract the £100 poll tax levied on coloured races in "White Australia". Tinworth enjoyed the joke and consented to make 100 of them with white faces! (plate 146). In a lecture delivered in the year following Tinworth's death, Shorter makes a special point of stressing the uncommercial attitude of Doulton to Tinworth and his independence from direct commercial pressures: "the last thing that Tinworth ever did was to perform any 'set definite task'."[5] No panel he ever conceived was ever ordered unless Tinworth himself accepted the commission after consultation with his individual patron, and the fact that nearly all his best known panels were still at Lambeth is direct evidence that they were in no way commercial, nor would he allow commercialism to influence him.

John Shorter was an enthusiast, "more Doulton-minded than Doulton himself,"[6] but he also encouraged others to buy panels — including Sir Samuel Way, Chief Justice of South Australia, who purchased the "Remorse of Herod." He was also perhaps instrumental in securing "The Greek Mother", a terra-cotta panel modelled in 1904/5 and now in Parliament House, Canberra, Australia (fig. 20). This panel, the inscription on which

Fig. 20. Terra-cotta panel: *"The Greek Mother"*.

reads "The Greek mother giving the shield to her son with the words 'either bring this shield back or be brought back upon it'," demonstrates that Tinworth was, although now in his sixty-first year, still able to manage epic subjects on a monumental scale. There is more than a superficial resemblance to the much earlier "Sons of Cydippe". He has, however, not repeated the error of flattening the forms to a degree which drains the earlier piece of much of its vitality. The well articulated array of figures in the foreground are sufficiently deeply modelled to allow the soldiers behind to be shaped in the round — giving a splendid sense of disciplined marching ranks. Figures are, however, somewhat static, standing in statuesque repose, without the justification in the Cydippe panel that the sons had been struck dead by the goddess Juno. The panel has some charming details, in particular the child carrying the votive offering to the altar.

Another enthusiastic and influential patron of Tinworth emerges at the time of the modelling of "The Greek Mother" panel. Richard W. Mould, Librarian at Southwark Central Library, began to correspond with Tinworth over the possible purchase of the Shakespeare memorial, upon which Tinworth was working without apparently having received a formal commission for it (fig. 21, see page 51). The surviving letters, dating from December of 1904 —

all from Tinworth to Mould — reflect a growing disappointment, almost despair, that so little encouragement was forthcoming from either public bodies or private patrons.

The Mayor and Aldermen of Southwark had taken preliminary steps to determine the cost of purchasing and publicly displaying an example of George Tinworth's sculpture as a tribute to their local celebrity. No doubt the non-religious nature of the Shakespeare memorial project was judged to have more general appeal and estimates were sought and received, but without a definite order being made. In the meantime Tinworth had almost finished the clay model and was proposing to fire it even though he still had no firm commission.

Finally, Tinworth despaired of the enterprise: "I often think whether there is any chance of my model Shakespeare coming to anything. The firm wishes me to stop making any more large panels as they cannot sell what I have already done, and I have not any commissions this two years. I wanted the firm to build a place to show them permanently but they will not. Has your museum been opened yet? I am beginning to loose hope for any future I am sorry to say." In spite of this, in a postscript Tinworth reports: "The large fountain has gone to [the] New Zealand Exhibition." The close-fisted attitude of the local council, and their failure to mark public pride in a local man, added to the increasing bitterness which over-shadowed Tinworth's last years — even turning him on occasion against Doulton's, his greatest benefactor and employer.

The full title of the autobiography which occupied Tinworth for the last few years of his life is worded "The Life of G. Tinworth, a London boy that became wheelwright and sculptor and for many years worked as an artist to the Doultons at their pottery High St Lambeth London from 1866." At the bottom of the page he declares acidly: "I want evil tongue people to know that I have written this book without the suggestion of the Doultons to do so."

A further demonstration of Richard Mould's concern and support for Tinworth deserves note. Over the Christmas period of 1910, and into January 1911, an exhibition of religious panels with early works — including the Bust of Handel in Portland Stone and the Wheelwright's Shop — was shown at Newington Public Library. Tinworth took a strongly paternal and protective interest in the safety of the exhibits: "I should like my things to come back to Kew by our van, not railway, as they will be safer that way." The show was a success although only locally advertised or noticed in the press. On January 9th, 1911, Tinworth gave a lecture with slides at Southwark Central Library on "Art work at Walworth and Lambeth." The press notice of this lecture suggests that the occasion was a triumph and quotes many of the spicier examples of Tinworth's humour and reparte. No doubt the writing of the autobiography which was proceeding at this time had sharpened Tinworth's perception of himself as a "character" and contributed to a more extrovert public face. Richard Mould continued to press for adequate local recognition of Tinworth and eventually was rewarded by the presentation by Doulton of "The Jews Making Bricks in Egypt", installed after Tinworth's death in the Cuming Museum, Walworth Road. Edmund Gosse unveiled the panel.

Tinworth had lived since his marriage in the commuter suburb of Kew, travelling to work by train from Kew station until the day he died. Maze Road, where he lived, is appropriately named, for it has a curiously convoluted right-angled configuration, lying in the centre of a network of well-tended semi-detached or terraced lines of properties. The River Thames forms a natural northern boundary and Kew Gardens is within easy walking distance. Tinworth owned No. 8 and in his will, dated 12th November, 1904, he left the property to his wife and, after her death, to his sister-in-law Ellen

Fig. 21. Portrait of George Tinworth working on the model for the Shakespeare Monument.

Digweed and his brother Thomas. It is evident that his wife Alice had become an invalid and that her unmarried sister Ellen lived with them, acting as housekeeper. The house, a simple two-storied late-Victorian brick structure has a small front garden and a charming plain wooden balcony projecting from the facade. Across the road the houses were larger, more elaborate, and later in date.

Tinworth was ailing throughout the Summer of 1913, complaining of cold and keeping a fire in his room: "He would sit in front of the fire of an evening covered with a shawl." He had characteristically refused to see a doctor. Autumn was approaching and in early September his health further deteriorated. On Wednesday, 10th September, he was unable to eat his breakfast, saying that a funeral had upset him. Ignoring his sister-in-law's advice, he insisted on taking the train to his studio at Doulton's. He left the house at 8:10 a.m. and was found dead in the train when it arrived at Putney Station at 8:40 a.m. The cause of death was a heart attack brought about by over-exertion. An elusive oral tradition has it that he chased boys from an orchard en route to the station. If that was so, it would be a sadly ironic note upon which to end the life of a man who, although childless, adored children and portrayed them with a warm affinity of feeling, identifying with their adventures and childish pranks.

Tinworth's death was extensively reported in the national and local press: "Death of Famous Sculptor Genius of Walworth who Rose from Poverty" *(Star)*; "Famous Sculptor Dead. Triumph of Genius over Poverty" *(Daily Citizen)*; "Death of Famous Sculptor. Rise to Fame of a Poor Walworth Boy" *(Daily News)*. Obituaries followed in most of the national newspapers, mainly recounting the familiar story of Tinworth's early struggles: his recognition by Ruskin and Gosse, his work for Doulton's and, for light relief, spiced with humorous anecdotes of his marvellous directness of speech and unconventional behaviour. One such story which does not appear elsewhere was recounted in the *Daily Chronicle*: "He once said that his finest piece was a production called 'Preparing for the Crucifixion', but when asked where it was, he would only vaguely answer 'Stowed away'."

Amongst the mourners at the funeral was Robert Wallace Martin, the long estranged childhood friend whose view of Tinworth had been soured by jealous rivalry. Serious critical evaluation of Tinworth's achievement had naturally enough been laid aside by most of the reporters and commentators who had favoured the "Romantic Story of a Wheelwright Sculptor" *(Titbits)* instead. *The Times* obituary was an exception to this. Following a summary of Tinworth's life and major works, *The Times* Art Critic (who was in those days anonymous) delivered a devastating evaluation of his qualities and limitations, which had remained unchallenged until 1960 when Charles Handley-Read, the pioneer re-appraiser of things Victorian, in two articles in *Country Life*[7] stripped prejudice away and looked afresh at Tinworth's quality as sculptor and potter.

The critical appraisal delivered by *The Times* Art Critic cannot be lightly dismissed as a typical piece of anti-Victorian prejudice; it contains enough truth to be valid today:

"There is a kind of primitive simplicity in some of his groups which makes them at least amusing and he is always at his best when he is least pretentious. But he had not enough of the true sculptor's curiosity about form and structure to make his work really inventive. He often imitated living people very well but, though he could also group his figures with some skill and some dramatic power, they remain rather life-like puppets than forms full of life of Art. And when he became more ambitious his lack of structural sense was obvious. His smaller works are his best; and they are interesting as attempts to enlarge the range of sculpture and to obtain new motives for design; but he was not a great designer any more than he was a great master of form. Yet he did better than many much more ambitious sculptors because he was a craftsman set definite tasks by his employers and because he was content to perform those tasks as well as he could."

The statement by *The Times* Critic that Tinsworth was "set definite tasks" by Doulton is contrary to the evidence of contemporary commentators and of Tinworth himself. It was clearly a matter of some sensitivity to Tinworth — whose comment on the title page of his autobiography has already been quoted. It is a remarkable feature of the relationship between Tinworth and his employers that so little direct influence was exerted upon him. Yet the debilitating consequence of such a continuous and benevolent patronage is a legitimate subject to raise. Tinworth continued to create religious panels long after public interest and support had dwindled away. The relatively unexploited potential of the humorous and secular pieces might have been served better by a stronger commercial drive.

Chapter Five

Assessment and Appreciation

During Tinworth's working lifetime an adventurous national school of Sculpture had emerged in England. The movement was given the title of the "New Sculpture" in recognition of its emphasis on non-classical and untraditional forms. It flourished from the late 1870's until the end of the first decade of the twentieth century. The principal exponents of the style, too old by the time of the Great War to fight in it, lived on to create the many hundreds of war memorials which survive today as the movement's final epitaph. On the continent, a similar shift of style in the last quarter of the nineteenth century developed rapidly into more experimental, non-naturalistic modes. By the time of Tinworth's death, representational sculpture had become unfashionable in Europe and the avant-garde in art generally had taken the stage.

In seeking to find a place for George Tinworth amongst his fellow artists, the possiblity of links with the New Sculpture and his contemporaries generally should be considered first. Gosse, in 1883, found no connections at all with the sculptor's fellow artists: "If we are called upon to decide what is the most prominent characteristic of George Tinworth, we might perhaps be inclined to answer isolation from all the other English artists of his time . . . we find ourselves at a loss to classify [the art of Mr. Tinworth]; it stands apart from all the traditional divisions of fine art, not so far apart, indeed, as to be eccentric or monstrous, but far enough to be outside the two main orders of painting and sculpture."[1] Eleven years later in a series of articles in the *Art Journal*, Gosse wrote another account of the New Sculpture, but this time omitted all mention of Tinworth.

In 1901, Marion H. Spielmann, the editor of *The Magazine of Art*, and a leading art critic, published in book form the first full account of recent trends in British sculpture.[2] He takes a broader view of the subject than Gosse did in his earlier *Art Journal* articles — giving Tinworth detailed attention. However, he cannot see him fitting in, for Tinworth's works are: "Symbols rather than sculptures seriously to be reckoned amongst the art of the day."[3]

In 1968, the Fine Arts Society mounted an exhibition "British Late 19th Century Sculpture", which included several pieces by Tinworth. The catalogue[4] contained an introduction by Lavinia Handley-Read, the first account to consider the sculpture of the period in any detail since Spielmann in 1901, although Eric Underwood had written a short general history of English sculpture in 1933.[5] Neither of these more recent authors, however, makes any reference to Tinworth in their surveys of the period.

The first full modern consideration of Tinworth as a sculptor was published in two articles in *Country Life* in 1960. The author, Charles Handley-Read, had, with his wife Lavinia, formed an important and influential collection of late nineteenth and early twentieth century fine and decorative arts.[6] Their combined scholarship played a crucial role in the re-evaluation of the period taking place during the 1960's and 1970's. At the time of the *Country Life* articles it was customary, indeed expected, that any consideration of "Victoriana" should be couched in language demonstrating a hostile or patronising attitude to the art of the period. In refreshing contrast, Charles Handley-Read approached the task of evaluation with a sympathetic understanding and admiration for what Tinworth had achieved. The views expressed in those articles are incorporated where appropriate into what follows.

The work of Tinworth falls into three main categories: decorative work including pottery and the small animal and figurative groups; monuments and large scale exhibition pieces; and finally, the religious terra-cotta panels and associated maquettes — together with occasional secular works in the same vein. Each of these categories in some degree contains its own criteria for critical evaluation; it is therefore necessary to deal with them separately.

Undoubtedly the groups of animals, particularly mice, performing or representing human situations, have been the most generally admired of all George Tinworth's creations. They were done, it seemed, entirely for relaxation and were designed to give pleasure and amusement to his friends, notably Henry Doulton and his family. Released temporarily from the solemn business of seeking out biblical truths, Tinworth's sense of humour and his acute perception of the frailty of human dignity are given full rein.

The use of animals in painting, writing, illustration and sculpture to satirise or reflect upon human action or attitudes was a favourite device in the nineteenth century. England, with its intense feeling for domestic animals, its "humanitarian" concern for the welfare of bird and beast, and the growing awareness of the need to study and conserve the world of living creatures, was a natural centre for such anthropomorphic devices. In painting, Queen Victoria's favourite animal portrayer, Edwin Landseer was pre-eminent; in literature, the mathematics teacher and amateur photographer, the Reverend Dodson, produced in the 1860's and 1870's (under the pen name of Lewis Carroll) first "Alice in Wonderland" and then its sequel, "Alice Through the Looking Glass." Both works were teeming with anthropomorphic creatures of every type and character — with their appearance defined with masterly conviction by the illustrator Tenniel. The subject of anthropomorphic art is explored more fully by the author when considering the grotesque Martin Birds of Robert Wallace Martin.[7]

In sculpture, both Martin and Tinworth excelled in the field of portraying animals behaving as humans, but each revealed his contrasting personality with disconcerting clarity. Robert Wallace Martin's grotesque Martin Birds are creatures of sinister and evil character; their wickedness is revealed in cruelly contorted, twisted features; they are victims of a malevolent creator. In contrast, Tinworth's mice, frogs, monkeys are amiable, friendly creatures much given to innocent, if misguided, enthusiasms. Dignity is frequently a casualty of some reckless undertaking or the outcome of a cruel twist of fate. In the "Cockneys at Brighton" (plate 104), the mouse family has unwisely put to sea and displays varying degrees of discomfort and apprehension at the turbulence of the waves. A similar family expedition of frogs in a carriage riding to the Derby is paired by a portrayal of the disconsolate return, their money lost in gambling on the horse races. It "Serves Them Right" according to the caption inscribed on the plinth (plates 120, 121). Sometimes childhood memories are stirred. In the "Playgoers" (plate 112), a small mouse peeps through a chink in the curtained Punch and Judy show booth, just as young George recalls himself doing, in his autobiography.

Charles Handley-Read somewhat dismissively considered that the animal groups and other similar small-scale humourous pieces "typify Tinworth's work at its most trivial level to be commented upon only for the sake of completeness". This view continued the critical devaluation of the more light-hearted aspects of the sculptor's work initiated by Gosse and reflected by most other contemporary critics. Such an attitude can no longer be supported. The Harriman-Judd collection has many examples of these enchanting pieces which demonstrate a masterly control and exploitation of the genre. Although over-shadowed by his large scale work, the animal groups belong to a long and vigorous tradition of English popular decorative pottery. For vitality and sheer delight they have few equals. Tinworth's pieces, when seen within that tradition, represent a consummate level of achievement in the genre.

Associated with the animal group are those incorporating children. Like other relatively small and vulnerable creatures, these youngsters, mainly boys, engage in activities somewhat beyond their physical statue — dressed as Roman legionnaries, they stand guard beside a column shaped candlestick (plate 134). The series of "Merry Musicians" (plate 146), of which almost sixty different types and variants have been recorded, personifies the ecstatic vigour and enthusiasm of youth with marvelous invention and ingenuity. "The Swimming Bath" (plate 137) shows the acuteness with which Tinworth observed and remembered his own childhood. He recalls in his autobiography, while swimming in the river, horseplay involving getting a ducking and having his hair pulled. He became aware for the first time of how his poorly clothed companions, relieved of their disfiguring garments, were transformed into lithe, muscular and graceful figures. He describes a ragged youth stripping off to swim: "I could not help seeing the great contrast for he was a fine figure when he had his clothes off."

Tinworth's attitude to the unclothed human body was somewhat ambiguous. Gosse faces the issues squarely: "Mr. Tinworth has a variety of Puritan foibles, which would surprise us in the nature of a sculptor, if they were not so manifestly proper to the nature of this particular man. He avoids, with great determination, all occasions on which he might be permitted to introduce the nude figure, and in those rare instances where he has employed it, the body seems studiously spare and unattractive. To his devout and simple mind a sense of asceticism is suitable in contemplating the finite body of fallen man, and while he avoids, on one side, the love of Roman art for what is hideous in the human frame transfigured by suffering, he has no sympathy whatever with the pagan feeling for physical loveliness or the rosy plumpness of imperturbable youth."[8]

There is no direct evidence of Tinworth's sexual attitudes, for his autobiography makes no reference to the subject. Indeed, his wife Alice and their childless marriage are not mentioned in it. It was, however, generally supposed that his narrow religious upbringing had suppressed that "pagan feeling" so eloquently described by Gosse. Stories that he had fled in shocked dismay from the naked Venus de Milo in the Louvre were clearly wrong according to the account in his autobiography already quoted. There are occasional portrayals of the naked or semi-naked female body, notably in his portrayal of Adam and Eve where he could scarcely avoid it; otherwise, his women are demurely clothed and somewhat matronly. There are several examples in the Harriman-Judd collection, including the "Tambourine Player" (plate 154) and "The Seasons" (plates 156-59), where the women are clad in simple shifts. There is one unusual example of a nude — a circular plaque of a seated women apparently painting or modelling a small statuette (plate 140). The complete lack of any erotic feeling, or indeed any real sympathy for the female body in these pieces, suggests that Gosse was at least partially right in his views.

A complete contrast is evident when the male body is portrayed. Tinworth had undertaken a full academic training based on the study of the human form. Several episodes in the account of his days at the Royal Academy Schools recall friendly and informal exchanges with the male models, and he continued to use models throughout his career. Indeed, the sensual feeling of real flesh and muscle inside his clothed male figures (the Roman soldiers notably), is a striking feature of many of the terra-cotta panels. The constraint he undoubtedly felt in portraying the female body found release in the more articulated contours of the male form. In this respect he identified with the dominant tradition of sculpture, which has always favoured the muscular body as against the softly contoured.

The final aspect of Tinworth's small scale decorative work to be considered is the pottery. Tinworth was never a potter in the sense that he threw and raised pots on the wheel, although he designed the shapes of many of the pots which were then made under his direction . An immediate critical problem arises. According to present-day orthodoxy, the process of making, decorating, glazing and firing should, as far as possible, be the work of one individual. The division of labour which allowed the decoration of the pot to be divorced from its making and, indeed, from the colouring and detailed embellishment, was taken for granted in the nineteenth century pottery industry. It was not until the 1880's and 1890's that a genuine studio pottery movement developed in Europe. In England, the Martin Brothers came nearest to fulfilling those aims, although the brothers divided the tasks of throwing, modelling, decorating and colouring between themselves and their assistants in much the same way as in industry, albeit on a smaller and more intimate scale.

Certain Doulton artists, notably Mark Marshall and Frank Butler, amongst Tinworth's contemporaries, developed a more integrated approach and appear to have operated very close to the studio model, although within a factory environment. Tinworth, however, was content with decoration and left the detailed work and the application of colour to others. Within those confines his sense of pattern is remarkable. John Sparkes discussed it with eloquent enthusiasm in the Society of Arts lectures already quoted. The Harriman-Judd collection contains splendid examples of the pottery decoration from Tinworth's best period. The spiralling seaweedlike form is capable it seems of almost infinite variation. It should be noted that an essential principle underlying the artist designed pottery at Doulton's was that each piece or pair was unique. Unfortunately, even Tinworth's invention flagged under the strain of producing many thousands of variants, and the later work sometimes lacks the exuberant vigour of those first pieces.

The second main category of work to be considered is the one which includes the monuments and large scale exhibition pieces. The Harriman-Judd collection contains a most remarkable example of the latter. The "History of England" vase (plate 52) must rank as one of the largest, most original and complex hollow sculptures in the history of pottery. It had several somewhat less ambitious precursors, notably the one exhibited at Philadelphia in 1876 (figure 7); otherwise it is difficult to trace an exact equivalent from any past style — the closest being the "Gres de Flandres" ware already described. Like the Philadelphia piece, the "History of England" vase was intended for exhibition in America, at the Chicago World's Fair of 1893. The scenes from English history which run in a continuous band round the body of the vase are full of lively incident (plates 53-55) and in many ways parallel the early experimental saltglaze pieces he made for the ebonised cabinet (figure 6).

The scenes also resemble, although on a smaller scale, the tableau on the equally remarkable fountain first exhibited at the Paris International Exhibition of 1878 (figure 11) and described in detail in the Chronology of Principal Works. Charles Handley-Read, thinking that it had been destroyed, imagined it to be "not much less than twenty feet high." Fortunately, the fountain survives and has been recently exhibited, although it turns out to be considerably smaller than the contemporary engraving suggested (upon which Handley-Read had based his judgment). It is an original, indeed eccentric concept and, seen in full operation with water rushing and gushing from the most improbable but logical places, it is overwhelmingly impressive. Of all Tinworth's early works, the fountain must represent the most effective and successful combination of his many-sided qualities. With more discriminatingly critical encouragement it could have heralded a series of equally adventurous and original projects.

Throughout his career, Tinworth undertook major public monuments, notably the Lord Shaftesbury, Samuel Morley, Charles Spurgeon and Henry Fawcett memorials already described. These men, eminent, philanthropic and pious, were fit subjects for Tinworth and he devoted much serious thought and great labour to them. In many way they are successful. The portraits, either in relief or fully in the round, are good likenesses, well achieved in the academic sense; indeed, he was an extremely competent portrait sculptor (plate 152). The other features, usually taking the form of relief panels portraying episodes from the life of the man commemorated, are well chosen and executed. However, for memorials to be finally accorded any significant artisitic value, there is an extra requirement which cannot be assessed in such measured terms. Unfortunately, the Tinworth pieces fail that final test precisely because he adopted such a conventional academic approach. A stroke of original genius similar to that which produced the fountain might have given the monuments a power to fire the imagination and truly reveal the qualities of the man commemorated. This essential ingredient in any assessment of sculptural worth will be considered afresh when the last and most considerable category of Tinworth's work is assessed.

The third category includes the large terra-cotta panels and other associated religious works — together with the occasional secular panels Tinworth carried out. Tinworth himself would have wished, indeed expected, to be judged by these large scale finished works with their elaborately conceived panoramas of teeming humanity rather than by his sketches. Contemporary critics were in accord with that expectation and devoted most of their attention to the major religious terra-cottas. Spielmann is notably less enthusiastic about them than Gosse had been: "Apart from the legitimate designs for pottery and the like, dramatic high relief panels with numerous figures on a small scale have absorbed the energies of Mr. Tinworth. The popularity of these is out of all proportion to their sculptural merits. But it cannot be denied that in the spirit that inspires them, and in the deep religious sentiment with which they overflow, there is ample justification for the public favour. Not for their art's sake, but for the vivid drama and intense passion with which the subjects are presented, they go straight to the heart of the devout or the unsophisticated spectator. They are often rugged in their force; naif almost primitive, in their conception and handling and so sincere that we are restrained from an occasional smile at the archaisms and the treatment by the perfect sincerity of the modeller."[9]

The "naif almost primitive" quality described by Spielmann referred in the main to Tinworth's handling of relief and in particular to his failure to master the true nature of bas-relief. As already noted, both Ruskin and Gosse used all their influence to shift Tinworth towards a more convention and illusionistic form of relief modelling. Handley-Read comments, however, that: "The value of their influence may be doubted because, whatever exalted standards the critics had in mind for him, his work seems to have shown greater vigour and conviction when he ignored, or failed to understand what they were driving at... In other words he knew his limitations, how best to achieve his desired effects with the utmost force."[10]

Present day attitudes to sculpture have moved so far from the narrow categorisation of nineteenth century academic theory that the controversy over what constituted an acceptable method of dealing with figures modelled against a background now seems somewhat sterile. What matters today is the sense of vitality and life; the immediacy of the rapidly executed sketch; "full of life and zealous faculty" as Ruskin declares at the very start of his early advocacy of Tinworth.

Most difficult for the modern observer to accept in Tinworth's sculpture is the overt preaching hammered home relentlessly in the jumbled semi-literate bibilical quotations surrounding and sometimes across the panels. These demonstrate and underline the didactic purpose of the representation. To fundamentalist Christians such as Tinworth, every word of the Bible not only represented an eternal truth but also carried the power to forecast or "pre-figure" events; hence, the importance of the texts to each episode portrayed. Many people considered that the crude and untidy lettering disfigured the sculpture, but it must be stressed that these captions are integral to the purpose of the panels and are an essential part of their composition.

The maquettes for the Guards' Chapel lunettes (plates 69-85) and the early salt-glaze panels designed to be fitted into furniture (plates 65, 66) have true sculptural feeling, using the basic clay, in a very modern, direct way. These pieces also reveal how adventurously figures and objects are articulated and counterpointed across the surface of the panels. "The Casting Out of the Money Lenders"(plate 66), with its extraordinary device of the dove flying out of the frame away from the upturned table, and the central figure of Christ with the sweeping arc of his cloak, demonstrate how much spirit and confidence Tinworth was able to bring to such subjects at the start of his career. At the same time it is important to recognize that, in the larger more finished panels, Tinworth retains much of the brilliant articulation of surface, wealth and inventiveness of incident and richness of characterisation which are his chief qualities.

Spielmann continued his theme with the following comments: "Here indeed is the art for which Tolstoy sighs, so simple and clear that none can reprove the artist either with vanity, with a desire for technical display or with the determination which comes from over refinement."[11] In other words, a category of artist which is recognized and admired in Russia today. He is called a "Peasant Master". The term is used to describe the humble, unpretentious but consummate craftsman whose skills made the great imperial palaces possible and whose inventive ingenuity gave so much added quality to the grand design.

Tinworth was just such a master; at his best when least pretentious, but always consummately skillful. A great master with much of the quality of the Renaissance artists-craftsman in him. He was no great innovator and the grand design was usually beyond him. He belonged to no avant-garde movement or, indeed, to any other kind of artistic fraternity. But he stands out, in the midst of an age of brilliant innovation, for the sturdy quality of his solid and enduring craftsmanship.

CHAPTER 1

1. Manuscript in the Southwark Local Studies Library; London.
2. Letter from GT to Gosse: "Distinction of Officer of the Academy for designing the Doulton ware and in recognition of my services to public instruction and to the Universal Exhibition." E.W. Gosse archive; Leeds University.
3. Edmund W. Gosse: *A Critical Essay on the Life and Works of George Tinworth*. Fine Art Society; London, 1883.
4. Desmond Eyles: *The Doulton Lambeth Wares*. Hutchinson; London, 1975.
5. A person licensed to sell or appraise household furniture distrained for rent.
6. Letter to Sydney Greenslade 21.9.1913. Southall Reference Library; London.
7. Gosse; p. 8.
8. *The Times;* December 19th, 1907; p. 8.
9. Henry Weekes, R.A.; Sculptor.
10. John Henry Foley, R.A.; Sculptor.

CHAPTER 2

1. Edmund Gosse: *Sir Henry Doulton*. Hutchinson; London, 1970; p. 82.
2. Desmond Eyles: *The Doulton Lambeth Wares*. Hutchinson; London, 1975.
3. *The Art Journal*, Vol. 38; p. 153.
4. Now the Royal Society of Arts.
5. John Sparkes: *Notes on Lambeth Stoneware, Faience, Terra Cotta and other Pottery*. Doulton & Co., 1880; p. 34.
6. Now part of the Museum of the Royal Army Chaplaincy, Bagshot Park, Surrey.
7. The Doulton Story Exhibition. Victoria & Albert Museum; London, 1979.
8. Charles Handley-Read: *Country Life*, 1960 — quoting the French critic Emile Bergerat.
9. Edmund Gosse: *Sir Henry Doulton*. Hutchinson; London, 1970; p. 119.
10. J.A. Blaikie: The Tinworth Exhibition, *Art Journal;* 1883; pp. 178-10.

CHAPTER 3

1. A manuscript collection of pieces written or drawn by Doulton artists and circulated within the firm to contributing subscribers.
2. Edmund Gosse: *Sir Henry Doulton*. Hutchinson; London, 1970; p. 120.
3. Ibid. p. 121.
4. Ibid. p. 121 (Editor's footnote).
5. "Going to Calvary" — now in Truro Cathedral.
6. Gosse: *Sir Henry Doulton;* p. 155.
7. Erroneously stated to be 1887 in the Royal Doulton Exhibition Catalogue, 1979; Sydney, Australia.
8. Manuscript in the Royal Doulton archives.
9. Gosse: *Sir Henry Doulton;* p. 169.
10. Ibid. p. 159.
11. Ibid. p. 166.

CHAPTER 4

1. "George Tinworth at Work" in *The Young Woman,* a monthly Journal and Review c. 1895, and "The Bible in Terra Cotta" in *Sunday Magazine,* pp. 92-99, February 1897.
2. Desmond Eyles: *The Doulton Lambeth Wares*. Hutchinson; London, 1975; p. 110.
3. A set of the fourteen panels was subsequently presented by Doultons to the Lambeth Borough Council.
4. The John Shorter Collection is now in the Sydney Museum of Applied Arts & Science.
5. He was quoting from *The Times* Obituary.
6. Royal Doulton Exhibition Catalogue — Sydney, 1979; p. 10.
7. Charles Handley-Read: "Tinworth's Work for Doulton", 1.) Sermons in Terra Cotta, and 2). Salt Cellars & Public Statues. *Country Life,* London, Sept. 1 and 15, 1960; pp. 430, 431 and 560, 561.

CHAPTER 5

1. Edmund W. Gosse: *George Tinworth*. Fine Art Society; London, 1883; p. 23.
2. Marion H. Spielmann: *British Sculpture and Sculptors of Today*. Cassell and Company; London, 1901.
3. Ibid. p. 23.
4. *British Sculpture 1850-1914*. The Fine Art Society; London, 1968.
5. Eric Underwood: *A Short Story of English Sculpture*. Faber and Faber; London, 1933.
6. *Victorian and Edwardian Decorative Arts: The Handley-Read Collection*. Royal Academy; London, 1972.
7. Peter Rose: "The Grotesque Ceramic Sculpture of Robert Wallace Martin". *Decorative Arts Society Journal,* Volume 3; pp. 40-54.
8. Gosse: *Tinworth;* p. 28.
9. Spielmann: *British Sculpture and Sculptors;* p. 23.
10. Charles Handley-Read: "Tinworth's Work for Doulton". *Country Life;* London, 1960; p. 431.
11. Spielmann: *British Sculpture and Sculptors;* p. 23.

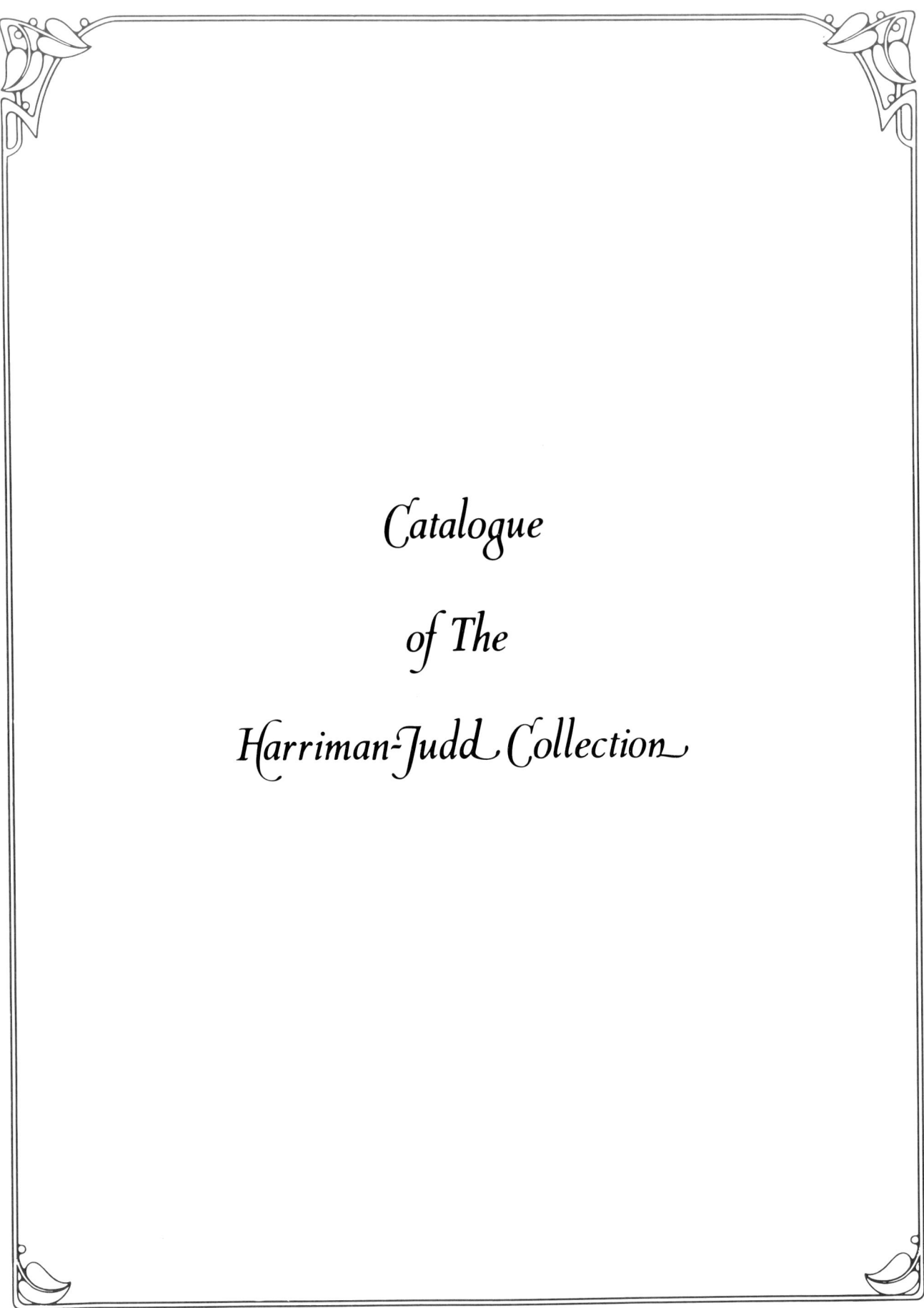

Catalogue

of The

Harriman-Judd Collection

Introduction

The pieces included in the following catalogue are all by George Tinworth working on his own or with assistants. In all cases where assistants were employed their identity is indicated either by name or symbol. Doulton products during George Tinworth's working life were usually marked in comprehensive fashion, providing information about date, type of clay, artist, senior assistant and junior assistant. All such information is included in the catalogue, although some discretion has been exercised over indicating the work of a junior assistant whose contribution has been judged to be minimal. In a fully illustrated catalogue it has not been considered necessary to provide a full written description of each object, although all inscriptions other than identification marks are fully transcribed, with spelling errors, stressed words, etc. retained when thought significant.

The monogram used by George Tinworth on the pots decorated by him and on the smaller pieces of sculpture is formed in several ways, showing that he must have explored different methods of forming the letters G.T. during the early period, when the Doulton oval mark did not include a date. Unfortunately, the inconsistencies revealed in comparing monograms on the later dated pieces suggest that any dates based exclusively on the form of the monogram should be treated with caution. The monogram nearly always appears on the main body of the piece, rather than on the base (which was the usual marking position for a Doulton artist). Unlike other artists, his mark is not accompanied by the incised number which is thought to represent some sequential record of work, carried out for stock-keeping purposes. Other identification marks such as the Doulton & Co. stamp are not transcribed, except for special or unusual ones; however, dating of the pieces is based on these marks unless otherwise stated.

The order of the catalogue has been determined by the type of work, chronological sequence, convenience of grouping and visual judgements. The last factor is judged to be of considerable importance by the sponsors who wish the catalogue to provide a visual experience worthy of the artist. For this reason the full catalogue details of the pieces are separated from the illustrations.

References in the catalogue to the two Doulton exhibitions which Richard Dennis presented in 1971 and 1975 in London have been abbreviated as follows:

Doulton Stoneware and Terra-cotta, 1870-1925 (Part I):   R.D.I.

Doulton Pottery from the Lambeth and Burslem Studios,
1873-1939 (Part II):   R.D.II.

Section I: Early Decorated Pottery

The group of pots in Section I is an example of the earliest period of George Tinworth's work as a pottery decorator for Doultons. The scrolled "seaweed" design which characterises most of his decorative surface treatment of pottery throughout his life, is already confidently managed. His taste for beaded reinforcement of the main thread of pattern is also apparent. Both the beading and the application of coloured slips would have been carried out by assistants under his general direction and supervision. Although not a trained potter, Tinworth would instruct the thrower to make pots according to the sculptor's own idea of shape and form.

PLATE 1 Vase: 13½" (35.6 cm) high. Saltglaze stoneware. Before 1872.

Incised G.T. monogram on base. Assistant's initials S.G. for Sarah Gathercole who was regularly associated with the artist at this period.

PLATE 2 Jug: 10" (24.5 cm) high. Saltglaze stoneware. Before 1872.

Incised G.T. monogram on base. Unidentified assistant's initials.

(Marks: Example "A")

PLATE 3A Vase: 7¾" (19.4 cm) high. Saltglaze stoneware. Before 1872.

Incised G.T. monogram on side. Inscribed on base "Weir" together with an impressed letter "C." Impressed letters were used to denote the clay type.

(Marks: Example "B")

PLATE 3B Jug: 10½" (26.4 cm) high. Saltglaze stoneware. Before 1872.

Assistant's initials S.G. for Sarah Gathercole together with an impressed letter "C" (see above). Although unsigned the jug is undoubtedly by Tinworth.

PLATE 4 Vase: 10½" (26.4 cm) high. Saltglaze stoneware. Before 1872.

Incised G.T. monogram on base. Unidentified assistant's initials.

PLATE 5 Jug: 12¼" (31.4 cm) high. Saltglaze stoneware. Before 1872.

Incised G.T. monogram on base. Assistant's initials for Sarah Gathercole.

PLATE 6 Vase: 9½" (24.5 cm) high. Saltglaze stoneware. Before 1872.

Assistant's initials S.G. for Sarah Gathercole together with an impressed letter "J." Although unsigned, the vase is undoubtedly by Tinworth.

PLATE 7 Jug: 10½" (26.4 cm) high. Saltglaze stoneware. Before 1872.

Assistant's initials S.G. for Sarah Gathercole together with an impressed letter "M." Although unsigned, the jug is undoubtedly by Tinworth.

Section II: Middle Period Pottery

The vases, jugs, candle holders and other small objects in this section occupy a period of roughly ten years between the mid-'70s and mid-'80s. George Tinworth was in his thirties and at the peak of his achievement. Some of his finest and most ambitious projects were undertaken at this time, notably the Paris Exhibition fountain, the Guards' Chapel wall reliefs, and many other major works. Critical acclaim was showered upon him and in consequence his personal confidence was at its peak. The freedom and directness which gives a "studio pottery" quality to the earlier pieces are replaced by a more controlled, refined and elaborated technique. Figures of putti and other small creatures are sometimes incorporated in the designs; these are assumed to have been modelled by George Tinworth, although casts from these small models are frequently found on pieces where another artist has made the principal contribution. A small group of such pieces is included in this section. Tinworth, in common with other Doulton artists, usually designed his vases in pairs; where there is a significant variation between the pots in a pair, both are shown; otherwise, one only is illustrated.

PLATE 8   Vase: 12" (30.4 cm) high. Saltglaze stoneware. Dated 1875.

Incised G.T. monogram on side. Unidentified assistant's monogram.

PLATE 9   Vase: 10½" (26.4 cm) high. Saltglaze stoneware. Dated 1875.

Incised G.T. monogram on side of base. Assistant's impressed mark for Mary Goode.

PLATE 10   Vase: 12¾" (32.4 cm) high. Saltglaze stoneware. Dated 1875.

Incised G.T. monogram on side. Assistant artist's incised initials for Eliza L. Hubert.

The seahorse handles are characteristic of George Tinworth.

PLATE 11   Vase: 9½" (24.5 cm) high. Saltglaze stoneware. Dated 1875.

Incised G.T. monogram on side. Assistant artist's incised monogram for W. Baron.

One of a pair.

The winged lion masks forming the handles to the vase are characteristic of George Tinworth.

PLATE 12   Vase: 8½" (20.9 cm) high. Saltglaze stoneware. Dated 1875.

Incised G.T. monogram on side of base. Unidentified assistant's mark.

The winged figures forming the handles to the vase are characteristic of George Tinworth.

PLATE 13   Vase: 18″ (45.5 cm) high. Saltglaze stoneware. Dated 1877.

Incised G.T. monogram on side. Unidentified assistant's incised initials S.E.G.

One of a pair.

This pair of very large vases was purchased in France c. 1970 by an English collector. They may have originated from the Paris exhibition of 1878.

PLATE 14   Vase: 9¾″ (24.7 cm). Saltglaze stoneware. Dated 1878.

Incised G.T. monogram on side. Assistant's mark for Fanny Clark.

One of a pair.

PLATE 15   Vase: 10⅛″ (25.8 cm) high. Saltglaze stoneware. Dated 1877.

Incised G.T. monogram on side. Assistant artist's incised initials for Eliza L. Hubert.

One of a pair.

PLATE 16   Vase: 13¾″ (34.8 cm) high. Saltglaze stoneware. Dated 1877.

Incised G.T. monogram on side. Unidentified assistant's incised initials S.E.G.

PLATE 17   Vase: 9½″ (24.2 cm) high. Saltglaze stoneware. Dated 1876.

Incised G.T. monogram on side. Assistant artist's incised monogram for Mary Thomson.

One of a pair.

PLATE 18   Vase: 9½″ (24.2 cm) high. Saltglaze stoneware. Dated 1876.

Incised G.T. monogram on side. Assistant artist's incised monogram for Mary Thomson; also a junior assistant's mark for Kate Giblin.

LEMONADE JUGS

The following pieces, all jugs of similar form, demonstrate the extraordinary variety of pattern George Tinworth achieved from the basic seaweed-like scrolling decoration he favoured throughout his career. The examples in the collection are all dated between 1874-1879 and were intended to be used for lemonade or a similar refreshment. It is assumed that most jugs were supplied with matching beakers, one of which survives (see PLATE 27).

PLATE 19   Lemonade Jug: 17¼″ (43.7 cm) high. Saltglaze stoneware. Dated 1878.

Incised G.T. monogram on side. Assistant artist's incised initials for Eliza L. Hubert.

The great size and weight of this jug and the lack of a pouring lip suggest that it was intended for exhibition rather than for any more practical purpose.

PLATE 20   Lemonade Jug: 9¾″ (24.7 cm) high. Saltglaze stoneware. Dated 1878.

Incised G.T. monogram on side of base. Unidentified assistant's mark.

PLATE 21   Lemonade Jug: 13″ (33.6 cm) high. Saltglaze stoneware. Dated 1877.
Incised G.T. monogram on side of base. Assistant artist's monogram for Mary Thomson.
The silver rim inscribed "March 1st, 1878" together with a monogram formed from the letters B.I.M.

PLATE 22   Lemonade Jug: 10½″ (26.7 cm) high. Saltglaze stoneware. Dated 1876.
Incised G.T. monogram on side. Assistant's initials for Sarah Gathercole.
The silver rim inscribed "Howell James & Co.; 5, 7 & 9 Regent St. London."

PLATE 23   Lemonade Jug: 11¾″ (29.9 cm) high. Saltglaze stoneware. Dated 1875.
Incised G.T. monogram on side.
The plated metal rim inscribed with a monogram formed from the letters H.R.T.

PLATE 24   Lemonade Jug: 9½″ (24.3 cm) high. Saltglaze stoneware. Dated 1877.
Incised G.T. monogram on side. Assistant's mark for Emma Martin.
Exhibited in R.D.I., No. 589.

PLATE 25   Lemonade Jug: 9½″ (24.4 cm) high. Saltglaze stoneware. Dated 1879.
Incised G.T. monogram on side of base. Assistant's mark for Emily Clark.
Exhibited in R.D.I., No. 591.

PLATE 26   Lemonade Jug: 11¼″ (28.7 cm) high. Saltglaze stoneware. Dated 1874.
Incised G.T. monogram on side. Assistant's initials for Sarah Gathercole.

PLATE 27   Lemonade Jug: 9¾″ (24.5 cm) high; Beaker: 5¼″ (13.5 cm) high. Saltglaze stoneware. Dated 1879.
Incised G.T. monogram on side of each. Assistant's mark for Rosina Brown.
Similarities of design and markings indicate that the beaker and jug were part of a set.

PLATE 28   Vase: 14″ (36.3 cm) high. Saltglaze stoneware. Dated 1880.
Incised G.T. monogram on side. Assistant's incised initials for Eliza L. Hubert.
One of a pair.

PLATE 29   Jug: 11″ (28 cm) high. Saltglaze stoneware. Dated 1877.
Incised G.T. monogram on side. Assistant's monogram for Emma Martin.
The Harriman-Judd collection contains several jugs of similar design, although none of the others is decorated by George Tinworth. There must, therefore, be some doubt about whether the distinctive shape and handle design are by him.

PLATE 30	Vase: 20″ (50.2 cm) high. Saltglaze stoneware. Circa 1885. Incised G.T. monogram. Otherwise unmarked. The pair to this vase was exhibited at the Royal Doulton Exhibition, Sydney, Australia, 1979 (L.37); illustrated on page 49 of catalogue. On this vase an assistant's mark for Emma Martin is recorded, but no Tinworth monogram. Like the vase in the Harriman-Judd collection, it is otherwise unmarked and undated. On stylistic grounds, the vases were probably produced in the middle to late 1880's for exhibition.
PLATE 31	Vase: 8¾″ (22.6 cm) high. Saltglaze stoneware. Dated 1875. Incised G.T. monogram on side. Assistant's incised initials for Emma Martin.
PLATE 32	Vase: 12¼″ (30.8 cm) high. Saltglaze stoneware. Dated 1878. Incised G.T. monogram on side. Assistant's incised initials for Eliza L. Hubert.
PLATE 33	Vase: 10″ (25.5 cm) high. Saltglaze stoneware. Dated 1875. Incised G.T. monogram on side of base. Assistant artist's monogram for Mary Thomson.
PLATE 34	Vase: 12″ (31.4 cm) high. Saltglaze stoneware. Dated 1882. Incised G.T. monogram on side. Assistant's monogram for Emma Martin.
PLATE 35	Cheese Board cover: 9″ (22.9 cm) high. Saltglaze stoneware. Dated 1879. Incised G.T. monogram on side. Assistant's incised initials for Eliza L. Hubert. Wooden base unmarked. There is no evidence to link cover and base, which, on stylistic grounds must be assumed to have been made at a separate time.
PLATE 36	Commemorative Vase: 9¼″ (23.7 cm) high. Saltglaze stoneware. Circa 1887. Incised G.T. monogram on side. Assistant's monogram for Emily Partington. The portrait is of Queen Victoria. The dates 1837 and 1887 are inscribed on the portrait reserves, which represent the young Queen Victoria on the one side and the older queen on the other.
PLATE 37	Inkwell: 4½″ (11.4 cm) high. Saltglaze stoneware. Dated 1875. Incised G.T. monogram on base. Unidentified assistant's initials E.B.
PLATE 38	Inkwell: 4½″ (11.4 cm) high. Saltglaze stoneware. Dated 1877. Unattributed initials C.A.O. Incised number 952. A similar inkstand was exhibited in R.D.I., No. 601; dated 1879 and attributed to Tinworth. Another inkstand of similar form, but with different patterning and incised B.J.Y. is in the Harriman-Judd collection but is not illustrated.

PLATE 39	Candleholder: 8″ (20.3 cm) high. Saltglaze stoneware. Dated 1876.
	No G.T. monogram visible. Unattributed assistant's initials C.A.O. Incised number 191.
	The pair to this candlestick was exhibited in R.D.I., No. 598; incised C.A.O. 190.
	The winged figures are from Tinworth moulds.
PLATE 40	Candleholder: 6½″ (15.8 cm) high. Saltglaze stoneware. Dated 1875.
	No G.T. monogram visible. Assistant artist's monogram for Eliza Simmance.
	A pair of similar candlesticks were exhibited in R.D.I., No. 597; also dated 1875.
	The winged figures are from Tinworth moulds and are similar to those shown in Plate 39.
PLATE 41	Salt Cellar: 4″ (10.1 cm) high. Saltglaze stoneware. Circa 1875.
	Incised G.T. monogram on base.
	A similar piece was exhibited in R.D.I., No. 602; dated 1874.
PLATE 42	Money box: 7¼″ (18.4 cm) high. Saltglaze stoneware. Circa 1875.
	Incised G.T. monogram on side. Unattributed assistant's monogram on base. No Doulton stamp.
	Inscribed on side "October 31" and monogram formed from the initials R.D. Possibly made for Ronald Doulton, the son of John Doulton Jnr.
PLATE 43	Vase: 17½″ (44.4 cm) high. Saltglaze stoneware. Dated 1882.
	Incised G.T. monogram on side. Assistant's incised initials for Eliza L. Hubert.
PLATE 44	Jardiniere: 7¾″ (19.7 cm) high. Saltglaze stoneware. Dated 1882.
	Incised G.T. monogram on side. Assistant's initials for Florence L. Hunt.
PLATE 45	Jardiniere: 7″ (18.0 cm) high. Saltglaze stoneware. Dated 1881.
	Incised G.T. monogram on side. Unattributed assistant's monogram.
PLATE 46	Bowl: 5″ (12.6 cm) high. Saltglaze stoneware. Dated 1881.
	Incised G.T. monogram on side. Assistant artist's monogram for Mary Thomson.
	The narrow collar shaped base suggests that this bowl was designed to be mounted.
PLATE 47	Plate: 7″ (18.0 cm) across. Saltglaze stoneware. Dated 1881.
	Incised G.T. monogram on upper surface. Unattributed assistant's initials on base.
PLATE 48	Jardiniere: 6½″ (16.5 cm) high. Saltglaze stoneware. Dated 1882.
	Incised G.T. monogram on side. Assistant's initials for Florence L. Hunt.

Section III: Late Period Pottery

With the exception of the History of England vase, this section is confined to a few examples of typical hollow-ware which George Tinworth continued to produce into the twentieth century.

PLATE 49　　Vase: 13″ (33.1 cm) high. Saltglaze stoneware. After 1902.

　　　　　　　Incised G.T. monogram on side. Assistant's initials for Florrie Jones.

PLATE 50A　　Vase: 10¾″ (27.3 cm) high. Saltglaze stoneware. After 1891.

　　　　　　　Incised G.T. monogram on side. Assistant artist's initials for Bessie Newbury.

PLATE 50B　　Vase: 12¾″ (32.4 cm) high. Saltglaze stoneware. Circa 1900.

　　　　　　　Incised G.T. monogram on side. Assistant artist's initials for Bessie Newbury. No Doulton stamp.

PLATE 50C　　Vase: 11″ (27.9 cm) high. Saltglaze stoneware. After 1902.

　　　　　　　Incised G.T. monogram on side. Assistant artist's initials for Bessie Newbury. One of a pair.

PLATE 51A　　Vase: 8¼″ (21 cm) high. Saltglaze stoneware. After 1902.

　　　　　　　Incised G.T. monogram on side. Assistant artist's initials for Bessie Newbury. One of a pair.

PLATE 51B　　Vase: 12″ (30.4 cm) high. Saltglaze stoneware. Dated 1903.

　　　　　　　Incised G.T. monogram on side. Unidentified assistant's mark.

　　　　　　　(Marks: Example "C")

PLATE 51C　　Vase: 9¼″ (23.7 cm) high. Saltglaze stoneware. After 1891.

　　　　　　　Incised G.T. monogram on side.

HISTORY OF ENGLAND VASE

PLATE 52　　"History of England" vase: 51½″ (131 cm) high. Saltglaze stoneware. Dated 1892.

　　　　　　Incised G.T. monogram and "H. Doulton & Co., Lambeth 1892" beneath middle tier of figures.

　　　　　　The circle of figures at the top represents an array of twenty British rulers and has incised beneath the figures: Caractacus, British; Boadicea, British; Caesar, Roman; Prince Vortigern; King Alfred, Saxon; Canute a Dane; Edward the Confessor; Henry II; Richard I; Henry III; Edward II; Edward III; Queen Philippa; Richard II; Henry IV; Henry V; Richard III; Henry VII; Queen Anne; George I, German.

　　　　　　The circle of groups of figures in the middle represents scenes from British history and has incised above — either in cartouche or in the arch: The Early Britons, Human Sacrifice, In the dark; Roman Invasion, B.C. 55; King Alfred and Bishop Asser; William the Conquerer and his sons; King John signing

Magna Charta, first step towards freedom; Edward I presenting first Prince of Wales to the Welsh; Henry VIII and Wolsey; Good King Edward VI going home; Cruel Queen Mary at prayers; Queen Elizabeth giving the ring to Lord Essex; James I and Guy Fawkes; Charles the First near the end of his trouble; Oliver Cromwell Protector tasting the misery of power; Charles II the Duke of Buckingham; James II escaping from Whitehall; William III landing in England; George III and Nelson; George IV and Queen Caroline; William IV the honest sailor; The Queen and Prince Albert, better times.

This highly ambitious sculptural vase was designed for exhibition at the Chicago World's Fair of 1893. Desmond Eyles illustrates an almost identical vase in its unfired state in his The Royal Doulton Lambeth Wares (plate 13). The vase was shown at "The Doulton Story" Exhibition at the Victoria and Albert Museum in 1979 (No. C.7) and is illustrated on page 13 of the Souvenir Booklet. The catalogue to the exhibition refers to "versions" of this vase which were exhibited at both Chicago and at the Imperial Institute Exhibition, London, 1894. It does appear likely that more than one version of the vase was produced, as the unfired vase illustrated by Desmond Eyles has small points of difference, and, according to the measurement given, was considerably larger.

PLATE 53   History of England Vase. Detail.

Top circle of figures. The central figures are: Caractacus, Boadicea and Caesar.

PLATE 54   History of England Vase. Detail.

Middle circle of groups of figures. The central group is: "The Early Britons, Human Sacrifice, In the Dark".

PLATE 55   History of England Vase. Detail.

Middle circle of groups of figures. The central group is: "Charles II and the Duke of Buckingham."

Section IV: Religious Panels

Undoubtedly, both George Tinworth and his contemporaries considered the religious relief terra-cotta sculpture to be his most important, technically brilliant and greatest artistic achievement. His reputation was built on the public admiration lavished on these works.

The belief that moral worth and artistic merit were inseparable was widely accepted by late Victorian society. It is perhaps a reflection of our present day values that many of the most ambitious religious works now seem over solemn, laboured and prosaic. Their didactic intention is made abundantly clear in the crowded biblical texts occupying every available flat surface surrounding, sometimes actually on the sculpture. The primitive vigour of the direct modelling, reinforced by the saltglaze firing process, gives his roughly executed sketches more present day appeal. The Harriman-Judd collection is of necessity limited in the number and size of finished terra-cotta sculpture, but it does contain a fine group of maquettes, notably the majority of those made as preliminary sketches for the Guards' Chapel lunettes. Sketch-books or preliminary pencil studies by Tinworth do not survive but, in any case, it is probable that he worked directly in clay from the start of the idea.

PLATE 56   Panel: Rebekah receiving gifts from Abraham's servant. 20½" (52 cm) wide, 13" (33 cm) high. Light-red terra-cotta. Dated 1888.

Incised "G. Tinworth 1888" and also G.T. monogram.

Inscribed above panel "And the servant took ten camels of the camels of his master and departed, for all the goods of his master were in his hand and he arose and went to Mesopotamia into the city of Nahor."

Inscribed below panel "Eliezer the servant of Abraham putting the bracelet on Rebekah."

Inscribed below edge of panel "If you want to please the ladies give them a piece of jewellery. If a good woman it is only adding jewel to jewel."

This panel is an example of the employment of the shallow relief modelling advocated by Ruskin. Mrs. Tinworth's diary for 1888 contains several references to this panel:

31 August: "...doing a panel of Rebekah with Abraham's servant bringing gifts."

29 October: "George finished Mrs. Buckland's panel of Rebekah receiving the bracelets from Abraham's servant."

19 November: "George has done another panel out of the mould of Rebekah receiving gifts of gold bracelets from Abraham's servant. He put underneath it, if you want to please the ladies give them a piece of jewellery but if they are good women it is only adding jewel to jewel."

PLATE 57   Panel: Jacob parting with Benjamin. 31½" (80 cm) wide, 11¾" (29.8 cm) high. Pale terra-cotta. Circa 1880.

Incised "H. Doulton & Co. Lambeth" and G.T. monogram.

Inscribed "Jacob parting with Benjamin, going the second time into Egypt to buy corn."

PLATE 58   Panel: The Sons of Cydippe. 60" (152.5 cm) wide x 30" (76.2 cm) high. Terra-cotta. Dated 1884.

Incised "H. Doulton, Lambeth. G. Tinworth (and G.T. monogram), January 1884."

Inscribed "The Sons of Cydippe from poem by Edmund Gosse, Acts XVII, Chap. VER."

A detailed account of this panel will be found in the Chronology of Principal Works.

PLATE 59   The Sons of Cydippe. Detail.

PLATE 60   The Sons of Cydippe. Detail.

The following four items are examples of a type of small terra-cotta panel which it appears was produced in some quantity over many years. However, each one contains a considerable amount of individual modelling with minor variations between versions of the same subject. The fully rounded figures stand out as in a tableau vivant.

PLATE 61   Plaque: Salome demanding the head of John the Baptist. 12″ (30.4 cm) wide, 5½″ (14 cm) high. Terra-cotta. Undated.

Incised "H. Doulton & Co. Lambeth: G. Tinworth" and G.T. monogram.

Inscribed above plaque "And the King was exceeding sorry. Yet for his oath sake and for their sakes which set with him, he would not reject her."

Inscribed below plaque "But the tongue can no man tame; it is an unruly evil full of deadly poison."

Inscribed under lower shelf "The tongue is only the servant of the mind."

PLATE 62   Plaque: The Slaying of the Innocents. 12″ (30.4 cm) wide, 5½″ (14 cm) high. Terra-cotta. Undated.

Incised "H. Doulton & Co. Lambeth. G. Tinworth" and G.T. monogram.

Inscribed above plaque "Then Herod when he saw that he was mocked of the wise men was exceeding wroth and sent forth and slew all the children that were in Bethlehem."

Inscribed below plaque "And on the side of there (sic) oppressors there was power; but they had no comforter."

PLATE 63   Plaque: The Entombment. 12″ (30.4 cm) wide, 5½″ (14 cm) high. Terra-cotta. Undated.

Incised "H. Doulton & Co. Lambeth. G. Tinworth" and G.T. monogram.

Inscribed above plaque "So they went and made the sepulchre sure. Sealing the stone and setting watch."

Inscribed below plaque "The earth with her bars was about me."

A similar panel is described by Gosse as "Sealing the Tomb."

PLATE 64   Plaque: A word to the Shepherds. 12″ (30.4 cm) wide, 5¼″ (14 cm) high. Terra-cotta. Undated.

Incised "H. Doulton & Co. Lambeth. G. Tinworth" and G.T. monogram.

Inscribed below plaque "Ye shall not enter the Kingdom of Heaven." The rest of the inscription is designed to be read as a diminishing spiral starting at the bottom left outer rim and running clockwise: "And Jesus called a little child unto him and set him in the midst of them and said verily I say unto you, except ye be converted and become as little children, ye shall not enter the Kingdom of Heaven. Therefore humble yourselves under the mighty hand of God that he may exalt you in due time."

(Marks: Example "E")

The following two plaques are closely related to the set incorporated in the ebonised cabinet (fig. 6) exhibited in the London International Exhibition of 1872 and now in the Victoria and Albert Museum.

PLATE 65　　　Plaque: "The Wise and the Foolish" 8¼" (21 cm) wide x 3¾" (9.5 cm) high. Saltglaze stoneware. Circa 1871.

Incised "H. Doulton, Lambeth. G. Tinworth" (cursive) and G.T. monogram.

Inscribed on surround "Let your loins be girded about and your lights burning: and Paraoh rose up in the night and there was a great cry in Egypt."

Inscribed on table in left panel "And when I see the blood I will pass over you."

(Marks: Example "D")

PLATE 66　　　Plaque: The casting out of the money lenders. 8¼" (21 cm) wide x 4" (10.2 cm) high. Saltglaze stoneware. Circa 1871.

Incised on bottom edge "H. Doulton & Co. Lambeth. G. Tinworth sc." and G.T. monogram. Assistant's initials S.G.

Inscribed on surround with key words stressed by using large size letters "and JESUS went into the TEMPLE of GOD and CAST out ALL them that SOLD and BOUGHT in THE TEMPLE: and OVERTHEW the TABLES of the MONEY CHANGERS and the SEATS of THEM that SOLD DOVES."

PLATE 67　　　Plaque: 6" (15.2 cm) diameter. Saltglaze stoneware. Circa 1877.

Incised "H. Doulton, Lambeth. G. Tinworth."

Inscribed at base "I will draw water for the camels also."

PLATE 68　　　Plaque: 6" (15.2 cm) diameter. Saltglaze stoneware. Circa 1877.

Inscribed at base "David would not drink of it but poured it out."

Inscribed on rim "To the Lord."

Although unmarked, the style of modelling together with the lettering support a Tinworth attribution.

THE GUARDS' CHAPEL MAQUETTES

The twenty-eight semi-circular terra-cotta panels commissioned by the architect, G.E. Street, for the rebuilt and decorated interior of the Royal Military Chapel (the Guards' Chapel) in Birdcage Walk, 1877/78, were almost all destroyed during the Second World War. Two surviving panels, together with "The Sowing of Tares" which was not installed in the Chapel, are now in the Museum of the Army Chaplaincy at Bagshot, Surrey. However, a record of their finished appearance survives in the catalogue produced by The Fine Art Society in 1883 accompanying the *Critical Essay on the Life and Works of George Tinworth* by Edmund W. Gosse. Only ten of the completed lunettes are illustrated, but all twenty-eight are fully described in the text. The seventeen maquettes in the Harriman-Judd collection are clearly early versions, possibly the first sketches for the series. One of the maquettes, however, does not have any equivalent subject in the final series, leaving a total of sixteen, or over half of the final series, surviving in sketch form.

Each maquette is incised "H. Doulton & Co., Lambeth, G. Tinworth" and each measures 12" (30.4 cm) wide x 9" (22.9 cm) high. Saltglaze red terra-cotta. Circa 1877.

PLATE 69　　　Inscribed "Adam & Eve in the Garden of Eden."

No. 1 "The Garden of Eden" in E.W. Gosse catalogue.

PLATE 70   Inscribed "Joseph being sold."
             No. 5 "The Selling of Joseph" in E.W. Gosse catalogue.

PLATE 71   Inscribed "Noah and his Family."
             No. 2 "The Ark" in E.W. Gosse catalogue.

PLATE 72   Inscribed "The Prodigal Son."
             No. 23: the same title in E.W. Gosse catalogue.

PLATE 73   Inscribed "Jesus Walking on the Sea."
             No. 24 "Christ Walking on the Sea" in E.W. Gosse catalogue.

PLATE 74   Inscribed "Naaman's visit to Elisha."
             No. 12 "The Visit of Naaman to Elisha" in E.W. Gosse catalogue.

PLATE 75   Inscribed "The Parable of the Lost Piece of Silver."
             No. 18 "Finding the Lost Piece of Money" in E.W. Gosse catalogue.
             Exhibited in R.D.I., No. 668.

PLATE 76   Inscribed "Jonah cast from the ship."
             No reference in E.W. Gosse catalogue.

PLATE 77   Inscribed "The Horse and his Rider hath He Thrown into the Sea."
             No. 6 "The Song of Miriam" in E.W. Gosse catalogue.

PLATE 78   Inscribed "The Fall of Jericho" and faintly impressed beneath "The Deliverance of Rehab."
             No. 8 "Joshua" in E.W. Gosse catalogue.

PLATE 79   Inscribed "Choosing Saul."
             No. 9 "The Finding of Saul" in E.W. Gosse catalogue.

PLATE 80   Inscribed "The Good Samaritan."
             No. 25: the same title in E.W. Gosse catalogue.

PLATE 81   Inscribed "Moses Lifting up the Brazen Serpent."
             No. 7 "The Brazen Serpent" in E.W. Gosse catalogue.

PLATE 82   Inscribed "Elijah and the Prophets of Baal."
             No. 11 "The Sacrifice on Mount Carmel" in E.W. Gosse catalogue.

PLATE 83   Inscribed "Raising of Jairus' Daughter."
             No. 26 "The Raising of Jairus' Daughter" in E.W. Gosse catalogue.

PLATE 84   Inscribed "Abraham and Isaac."
             No. 3 "The Offering of Isaac" in E.W. Gosse catalogue.

PLATE 85   Inscribed "David and Goliath."
             No. 10 "David Killing Goliath of Gath" in E.W. Gosse catalogue.
             Exhibited in R.D.I., No. 667.

Section V: Animal Groups

No greater contrast in mood and attitude can be imagined than between the high seriousness of the religious plaques and the frivolous humour of George Tinworth's animal groups. A fuller analysis of the anthropomorphic character of these pieces is to be found in the evaluation of his life and work. These pieces were much enjoyed by Tinworth's associates, particularly Henry Doulton himself who commissioned duplicate sets of many of them. Tinworth himself saw this side of his work as light-relief and would have found the modern day attitude, which places them on a higher level of appreciation than the religious panels, incomprehensible.

It is not clear how many versions of each idea were produced. Edward Salmon in *The Strand Magazine* in 1891 indicates that "Cockneys at Brighton" was produced in some quantity, and the "Mouse and the Currant Bun" continued in production well into the twentieth century. Most of the pieces display mould marks and, no doubt, were intended to be reproduced. The relative rarity of surviving pieces may perhaps be attributable to their undoubted appeal to children; the damaged nature of many of the survivors tending to confirm that supposition. The pieces are rarely dated but references suggest that they could have been produced at any time between the 1870's and 1890's.

PLATE 86 Clockcase: "Fables" 11¾" (29.8 cm) wide x 10¼" (26 cm) high. Saltglaze stoneware. Dated 1883.

Incised G.T. monogram on base of column; "H. Doulton, Lambeth" on side of plinth. Assistant artist's initials for Eliza L. Hubert.

Inscribed "Fables"; "The Pigeon and the Kite"; "The Two Rabbits"; "The Wolf and the Naughty Boy"; "Fox and Grapes".

A similar piece is described by E.W. Gosse on page 81 of his catalogue of the 1883 exhibition, although it is not referred to as a clockcase but as part of a collection of "miniature reliefs." R.D.I., No. 656 is similar, although constructed differently.

PLATE 87 Clockcase: "Fables." Detail.

"The Nurse and the Wolf"

Gosse's catalogue entry explains the fable: "Hearing a nurse threaten to throw a troublesome child to the wolf, that animal waited a long time in expectation of her doing so; but afterwards, when the nurse, to please the child, promised to kill the wolf, he retired, blaming himself for having put faith in the words of a woman."

PLATE 88 Clockcase: "The Menagerie". Detail of left side.

PLATE 89 Clockcase: "The Menagerie". Detail of right side.

PLATE 90 Clockcase: "The Menagerie". Detail of lower front.

PLATE 91	Clockcase: "The Menagerie" 9½" (24.2 cm) wide x 9½" (24.2 cm) high x 5¾" (14.5 cm) deep. Saltglaze stoneware. Circa 1885.
	Incised G.T. monogram on front. Assistant's mark for Emily Partington.
	Inscribed: "The Three Card Trick"; "The Wild Beast Show"; "The Wheel of Fortune".
	Exhibited in R.D.I., No. 657.
	Exhibited in *The Doulton Story* at Victoria and Albert Museum; illustrated on page 18 of the Souvenir Booklet.
PLATE 92	Menu holder: Musicians — 3½" (8.8 cm) high. Saltglaze stoneware. Circa 1885.
	Incised G.T. monogram on reverse.
	Indistinctly inscribed.
PLATE 93	Menu holder: "Organ Grinder." 3¼" (8.2 cm) high. Saltglaze stoneware. Circa 1885.
	Incised C.T. monogram on side.
	Inscribed "Organ Grinder".
PLATE 94	Menu holder: "The Conjurors" 3½" (8.8 cm) high. Glazed porcelain. Undated.
	Incised G.T. monogram on reverse.
	The unusual body used in this piece suggests that it may have been produced at the Doulton works at Burslem rather than Lambeth. See also Plate 96.
PLATE 95	Menu holder: "Organ Grinder" 3¾" (9.5 cm) high. Saltglaze stoneware. Dated 1885.
	Incised G.T. monogram.
PLATE 96	Menu holder: "The Conjurors" 3½" (8.8 cm) high. Saltglaze stoneware. Dated 1885.
	Incised G.T. monogram.
	Inscribed "The Conjurors." See also Plate 94.
	A similar group was exhibited in R.D.II., No. 301; dated 1886.
PLATE 97	Menu holder: "Potter" 3¾" (9.5 cm) high. Saltglaze stoneware. Circa 1885.
	Incised G.T. monogram on reverse.
	Inscribed "Potter".
PLATE 98	Menu holder: "Cornet Blowers" 3½" (8.8 cm) high. Saltglaze stoneware. Circa 1885.
	Incised G.T. monogram on reverse.
	Inscribed "Cornet Blowers".
	A similar group was exhibited in R.D.I., No. 648. There are marked differences in the placing and expressions of the mice performers.
PLATE 99	Menu holder: "The Quack Doctor" 4" (10.2 cm) high. Saltglaze stoneware. Circa 1885.
	Incised G.T. monogram on reverse.
	Inscribed "Mr. Home Leach. Quack Doctor".

PLATE 100   Menu holder: "Mouse Musicians" 3½" (8.8 cm) high. Saltglaze stoneware. Dated 1886.

Incised G.T. monogram on reverse.

Inscribed "Mouse Musicians".

A similar group was exhibited in R.D.II., No. 297; also dated 1886.

PLATE 101   Menu holder: "The Wheelwright" 3¾" (9.5 cm) high. Saltglaze stoneware. Dated 1886.

Incised G.T. monogram on reverse.

Inscribed "The Wheelwright".

The subject must have had particular appeal to Tinworth who, in his youth, followed the trade of wheelwright, like his father.

PLATE 102   Menu holder "The Sculptor" 4" (10.2 cm) high. Saltglaze stoneware. Dated 1886.

Incised monogram on reverse.

Inscribed "The Sculptor".

PLATE 103   Menu holder: "Painting" 3½" (8.8 cm) high. Saltglaze stoneware. Circa 1885.

Incised G.T. monogram on reverse.

Inscribed "Painting".

A similar group was exhibited in R.D.II., No. 298; dated 1886.

PLATE 104   Mouse group: "The Cockneys at Brighton" 4" (10.2 cm) high. Saltglaze stoneware. Dated 1886.

Incised G.T. monogram on reverse.

Inscribed "The Cockneys at Brighton".

PLATE 105   Tile: "Photography" 6" (15.2 cm) square. Saltglaze stoneware. Undated.

Incised G.T. monogram on concave surround of mouse group. Assistant's initials for Rosina Brown.

Inscribed "Photography".

PLATE 106   Mouse group: "Drunkards" 3¼" (8.3 cm) high. Saltglaze stoneware. Circa 1885.

Incised G.T. monogram.

Inscribed "Drunkards".

PLATE 107   A Frog and Mouse group: "The Steeplechase" 4½" (11.5 cm) high. Saltglaze stoneware. Undated.

Incised G.T. monogram on side.

The title of this piece is not visible; it is possibly covered by slip. A similar group was exhibited in R.D.I., No. 643. The frogs, however, were uncoloured. It is possible that the frogs are riding rats rather than mice.

PLATE 108   Mouse group: "Tea Time Scandal" 4" (10.2 cm) high. Saltglaze stoneware. Circa 1888.

Incised G.T. monogram on reverse. Assistant's mark for Emily Partington.

Inscribed on plinth "Tea Time Scandal".

This group appears to be the one exhibited in R.D.I., No. 641.

At least one other version is known. In Mrs. Tinworthy's diary for 1888 there is a reference to this group: "Monday, 30 January. George has designed three frogs on rock work for trial and some mice having tea called "Scandal". Tinworth designed a similar group but with human participants also called "Scandal". It is supposedly based on a visit to Mrs. Henry Doulton and her friends (illustrated in the Souvenir Booklet *The Doulton Story,* page 19). In his autobiography, George Tinworth refers to "a small group of mice in stoneware which I called 'Scandal' and when she (Mrs. Doulton) saw it she said it did not refer to her and I do not think it did."

PLATE 109 Paperweight: Mouse Flute player — 3½" (8.8 cm) high. Saltglaze stoneware. Dated 1884.

Incised G.T. monogram.

PLATE 110 Paperweight: Mouse on a Current Bun — 3" (7.6 cm) high. Saltglaze stoneware. Dated 1884.

Incised G.T. monogram.

PLATE 111 Paperweight: Mouse cornet player — 3½" (8 cm) high. Saltglaze stoneware. Dated 1886.

Incised G.T. monogram.

PLATE 112 Mouse group: "Playgoers" 5½" (14 cm) high. Saltglaze stoneware. After 1891.

Incised G.T. monogram.

Inscribed "Playgoers".

A similar group was exhibited in R.D.I., No. 642; dated 1886, assisted by John Broad. Several versions of this subject are known.

PLATE 113 Mouse group: "Niggers" 3¾" (9.5 cm) high. Saltglaze stoneware. Undated.

No G.T. monogram visible. Assistant's mark for Emma Shute.

Inscribed on plinth "Niggers".

A similar group was exhibited in R.D.I., No. 638.

PLATE 114 Spill vase: "The Pillars of Wealth" 4¼" (10.8 cm) high. Saltglaze stoneware. Undated.

Incised G.T. monogram.

Inscribed "The Pillars of Wealth, and Poverty Between".

A similar group was exhibited in R.D.I., No. 646. It was, however, inscribed "Homeless" and had only one pillar.

PLATE 115 Mouse group: "Waits" 5¼" (13.3 cm) high. Saltglaze stoneware. Undated.

Incised G.T. monogram on side.

Inscribed on house front "J. Mouse, Candle Consumer" and on plinth "Waits".

Although similar to a group exhibited in R.D.II, No. 300, there are marked differences. In the exhibited version, Mr. J. Mouse is pouring water over the mice musicians. In that version the plinth inscription is "Waits Water". It is probable that the two groups were intended as a pair.

PLATE 116　　Fob watch holder: 5½" (14 cm) wide x 4½" (11.5 cm) high. Saltglaze stoneware. Undated.

Incised G.T. monogram and "H. Doulton, Lambeth".

PLATE 117　　Mouse chess set: The Reds. Height of King 4¼" (10.7 cm). Cold-painted white clay. Circa 1885.

Incised G.T. monogram on King and Queen only. "Doulton" stamped on base.

Two complete chess sets are known to survive. Several individual pieces in saltglaze stoneware have also been recorded.

PLATE 118　　Mouse chess set: A game in progress.

PLATE 119　　Mouse chess set: The Blacks.

PLATE 120　　Frog group: "Going to the Derby" 4" (10.2 cm) high. Saltglaze stoneware. Circa 1885.

Incised G.T. monogram. Assistant's monogram for Jane Hurst.

Inscribed "Going to the Derby" and "To Epsom" on signpost.

A special fixing on the signpost suggests that this piece and its pair (121) were intended to be used as menu holders.

PLATE 121　　Frog group: "Returning from the Derby" 4" (10.2 cm) high. Saltglaze stoneware. Circa 1885.

Incised G.T. monogram. Assistant's monogram for Jane Hurst.

Inscribed "Lost and serve them right", and "To London" on signpost. Probably intended as a menu holder (see 120).

PLATE 122　　Frog group: "Jack in the Green" 5¼" (13.3 cm) high. Saltglaze stoneware. Circa 1885.

Incised G.T. monogram.

Inscribed "Jack in the Green".

PLATE 123　　Frog group: "Bicyclist" 4½" (11.5 cm) high. Saltglaze stoneware. Circa 1885.

Inscribed "Bicyclist"; otherwise unsigned.

An identical group was exhibited in R.D.I., No. 637; also unsigned.

PLATE 124　　Frog group: "The Public Library's Act" 5¼" (13.3 cm) high. Saltglaze stoneware. Circa 1884.

Incised G.T. monogram on reverse. No Doulton stamp.

Inscribed "In Memory of Public Library's Act".

The provision of Public Libraries was established in England by a Parliamentary Act of 1850. This was followed by several modifications and extensions to the regulations over the next half century. The event commemorated in this piece is likely to be the Public Library's Act of 28 July, 1884, which extended the original provisions to cover the relationships between libraries, Art Galleries and Museums, and Schools of Art.

PLATE 125　　Frog group: "The Football Scrimmage" 5″ (12.7 cm) high. Saltglaze stoneware. Circa 1885.

Incised G.T. monogram.

Inscribed "The Football Scrimmage."

PLATE 126　　Frog group: "The Football Scrimmage." Reverse view.

PLATE 127　　Animal group: "Safe Traveling" 6¾″ (17.2 cm) high. Saltglaze stoneware. Circa 1885.

Incised on base "Doulton Ltd., Lambeth"; G.T. monogram on side of plinth. Assistant's unidentified initials F.J.

Inscribed (twice) "Safe Travelling".

The following three items are based on Aesop's Fables. A group of these was included in the E.W. Gosse catalogue of the 1883 exhibition.

PLATE 128　　Fable group: "The Monkey" 4″ (10.2 cm) high. Saltglaze stoneware. Circa 1882.

No monogram visible.

Inscribed on reverse "Fable."

Inscribed on front of plinth under title "The Monkey that would be a King".

This piece illustrates the Aesop Fable "The Fox and the Ape". Described in E.W. Gosse catalogue, page 80.

PLATE 129　　Spill vase: "The Honeymoon" 4¾″ (12.1 cm) high. Saltglaze stoneware. Dated 1880.

No G.T. monogram. Assistant's mark for Mary A. Thomson.

Inscribed "The Waning of the Honeymoon".

A similar group was exhibited in R.D.I, No. 450; unsigned but attributed to George Tinworth.

PLATE 130　　Frog dish: "The Ox and the Frogs" 3″ (7.6 cm) high x 7″ (17.8 cm) wide x 7″ (17.7 cm) deep. Saltglaze stoneware. Dated 1881.

Incised on base "H. Doulton, Lambeth, 1881" and G.T. monogram.

Inscribed "The Ox and the Frogs." Also a monogram H.L.D.

Exhibited in "The Doulton Story" at the Victoria & Albert Museum, 1979; illustrated page 18 of Souvenir Booklet. In the caption to the illustration it is suggested that this dish may have been intended as a present for the young Henry Lewis Doulton. The subject is the Aesop Fable "The Frog who would be as big as an Ox". Described in E.W. Gosse catalogue, page 79.

PLATE 131　　Monkey group: "A United Family" 4¾″ (12.1 cm) high. Saltglaze stoneware. After 1891.

Incised G.T. monogram. Impressed number 3598.

Inscribed "A United Family".

A similar group was exhibited in R.D.I., No. 639.

PLATE 132 Covered dish: "Monkey, Cats and Cheese" 6" (15.2 cm) high. Saltglaze stoneware. Dated 1882.

Incised G.T. monogram.

Inscribed "Monkey, Cats and Cheese".

This piece illustrates the Aesop Fable "The Cats and the Cheese". See E.W. Gosse catalogue, page 79.

PLATE 133 Plaque: Donkeys — 7½" (19 cm) high x 5½" (14 cm) wide. Saltglaze stoneware. Circa 1875.

Incised G.T. monogram twice on background; otherwise unmarked.

Section VI: Human Figures and Groups

Although portraying animals, mice in particular, stimulated George Tinworth to his sharpest barbs of humour, the closely observed portrayals of children demonstrate his warmth and sympathetic kindness to small vulnerable creatures most successfully. The Harriman-Judd collection contains many fine examples, including a representative group of individual boy figures from the Merry Musicians series and also one of Tinworth's strangest and most appealing concepts, "The Swimming Bath". His attempts to portray women suffer from the artistically inhibiting belief in the virtues of modesty and decorum and in consequence have a somewhat wooden depersonalised appearance.

PLATE 134 Candlesticks with Boy Soldiers — 12¾" (32.4 cm) high. Saltglaze stoneware. Undated.

Incised G.T. monogram on the shield.

Similar boy soldiers are used to flank a letter-rack exhibited in R.D.I, No. 623. They also resemble the boys in the Tennis clockcase (Plate 145).

PLATE 135 Seated Youth — 12¾" (32.4 cm) high. Saltglaze stoneware. Undated.

Incised G.T. monogram on the seat.

Inscribed "H. Doulton, Lambeth."

PLATE 136 Seated youth — 12¾" (32.4 cm) high.

A pair to Plate 135.

PLATE 137 "The Swimming Bath" 11½" (29.2 cm) high x 3¾" (9.5 cm) high x 6½" (16.5 cm) deep. Saltglaze stoneware. Undated.

Inscribed "G. Tinworth. The Swimming Bath. (A) Sketch" and G.T. monogram. No Doulton mark or date.

PLATE 138 "The Swimming Bath." Detail.

PLATE 139 "The Swimming Bath." Detail.

PLATE 140 Circular plaque with seated woman — 9½" (24.1 cm) diameter. Saltglaze stoneware. Undated.

Incised G.T. monogram on seat. Underneath are incised numbers, the letter "F" and other marks. There is no Doulton name however. The seated figure appears to be either painting or sculpting a small figurine.

PLATE 141A   Salt cellar with Boy Drummer — 3½″ (9.0 cm) high. Saltglaze stoneware. Circa 1885.

Incised G.T. monogram on reverse.

A similar piece is illustrated in R.D.I, No. 605.

PLATE 141B   Salt cellar with Boy Fowl Seller — 4″ (10.2 cm). Saltglaze stoneware. Circa 1885.

Incised G.T. monogram on reverse.

PLATE 142   Spill vase: Boy with two vases — 5¼″ (13.3 cm) high. Saltglaze stoneware. Circa 1885.

Although the piece is unsigned, it is attributed to Tinworth. This piece was exhibited in R.D.I., No. 606.

PLATE 143   Card holder: "The Telephone" 4½″ (11.5 cm) high. Saltglaze stoneware. Circa 1885.

Incised G.T. monogram on side.

Inscribed "The Telephone. Good News".

PLATE 144   Flower Holder: Cherubs riding seahorses — 4¾″ (12 cm) high. Saltglaze stoneware. Dated 1878.

Incised G.T. monogram on foreground. Assistant artist's monogram for Mary Thomson.

PLATE 145   Clockcase: Tennis Players — 10″ (25.4 cm) high. Saltglaze stoneware. Undated.

Incised G.T. monogram. Assistant artist's monogram for Eliza Simmance. Incised number 752 R.

The oval recess on top of the clockcase may have originally held a small, separately sculpted, decoration.

PLATE 146   A Band of Merry Musicians: Between 4″ (10.2 cm) and 5½″ (14 cm) high. Saltglaze stoneware.

A photographic record survives of the original clay models for fifty-five different figures playing thirty-seven different instruments. However, several variants and modifications of these are known, making the total number of distinct types higher. The pieces were in production from the 1880's onwards. They were moulded and then individually finished so that minor variations between seemingly identical subjects occurred throughout the period of production. The white faced boys were made for the Australian market, according to the contemporary account referred to in the text (pages 48-49).

All the pieces illustrated are incised with G.T. monogram and none is dated. The instruments played include a piano, accordion (2), violin (2), guitar, viola, tuba, trumpet (2), flute (2), double bass and mandolin.

PLATE 147   Musician: The Viola Player — 4¾″ (12 cm) high. Earthenware; glazed and part gilt. After 1892.

Incised G.T. on reverse. Painted assistant's mark.

An unusual example of a Tinworth piece in "Crown Lambeth" — a refined type of earthenware produced at Lambeth between 1892 and 1900.

PLATE 148   Boy Jester playing a mandolin — 7" (15.2 cm) high. Saltglaze stoneware. Undated.

Incised G.T. monogram and "H. Doulton, Lambeth".

Unidentified assistant's initials W.H.

Although a musician, this piece does not strictly belong to the set as it has a different type of base.

PLATE 149   The Banjo Player — 4½" (11.4 cm) high. Saltglaze stoneware. Undated.

Incised G.T. monogram.

There is a fixing on reverse for a menu holder.

The use of coloured slip, particularly the white, is unusual in the musician series.

PLATE 150   The Jester — 12½" (31.7 cm) high. Light red terra-cotta. Circa 1900.

Incised on plinth "The Art Union of London. The Jester by Geo. Tinworth".

The piece appears to be individually modelled, not cast. The inscriptions on the plinth are uncharacteristic of Tinworth's lettering and are almost certainly not by him. A model similar to this piece, possibly the same one, is visible in the photograph of George Tinworth working on the Shakespeare memorial. Twelve copies were made for The Art Union as prizes. One example was shown in the Paris Exhibition of 1900.

PLATE 151   The Boy Jester — 5" (12.7 cm) high. Saltglaze stoneware. Undated.

Incised G.T. monogram and "Doulton, Lambeth".

Although not a musician, this figure belongs stylistically to the group.

PLATE 152   Head of a Man — 18" (45.4 cm) high. Terra-cotta. Circa 1890.

Inscribed "G. Tinworth. H. Doulton & Co. Lambeth".

Although not positively identified, this portrait bust is likely to be a member of the Doulton family. In his autobiography Tinworth recalls that "I modelled Mr. Lewis Doulton's bust, only son of Sir H. Doulton, now Chairman of the firm." A comparison with the portrait of Henry Lewis Doulton drawn by Sir William Rothenstein in 1929 reveals strong similarities with the much younger man portrayed in the bust.

PLATE 153   Girl with Tambourine — 9" (22.9 cm) high. Saltglaze stoneware. Undated.

Incised G.T. monogram on reverse of seat.

PLATE 154   Tambourine Player — 15" (38.1 cm) high. Saltglaze stoneware. Undated.

Although unmarked, this figure is almost certainly by Tinworth.

The unfinished base suggests that the figure was intended to form part of a larger piece.

PLATE 155   Spill vase: Boy Cyclist — (22.8 cm) high. Saltglaze stoneware. Circa 1885.

Incised G.T. monogram on reverse. No Doulton mark visible.

Inscribed on milestone behind the bicycle "5 miles to London".

Four plaques: The seasons — 6½" (16.5 cm) wide x 12¾" (32.4 cm) high. Blue glazed stoneware. Undated.

Incised G.T. monogram.

These plaques are inscribed on the base:

PLATE 156   "Spring" (details as above).

PLATE 157   "Summer" (details as above).

PLATE 158   "Autumn" (details as above).

PLATE 159   "Winter" (details as above).

Four plaques: The Seasons — 8½" (21.6 cm) high x 4¼" (10.8 cm) wide. Saltglaze stoneware. Circa 1876.

The plaques were inscribed around the border:

PLATE 160A   "Seed Time: In the morning sow they seed".

PLATE 160B   "Summer Time: He that gathereth in summer is a wise son".

PLATE 161A   "Harvest Time: They joy before thee according to the joy in harvest".

PLATE 161B   "Winter Time: Summer and winter and day and night shall not cease".

A similar set of plaques was exhibited in R.D.I., No. 660. The exhibited set however, is not so finely modelled. There are also minor differences in the inscriptions. In George Tinworth's autobiography there is a reference to similar panels: "After I had been at Doulton's some time Lord Ronald Gower came into my room and bought four little panels — four boys representing the seasons in stoneware".

PLATE 162   Box with cover: "The Drunken Husband" 5¼" (13.3 cm) high. Saltglaze stoneware. Circa 1880.

Incised G.T. monogram on the plinth. Exhibited in R.D.I., No. 654. Illustrated in "The Doulton Story" Souvenir Booklet, page 19. This subject, taken from Aesop's Fables, is described by E.W. Gosse in his catalogue of the 1883 exhibition, page 79.

PLATE 163   The Drunken Husband: Detail.

PLATE 164   The Carpenter's Tools—3½" (9.0 cm) high. Saltglaze stoneware. After 1891.

No G.T. monogram. Assistant's mark E.H. and R.P. 162583.

A similar piece was exhibited in R.D.I., No. 607. Attributed to George Tinworth.

FIGURE I   Oval plaque: Self-portrait of George Tinworth — 5¼" (14.6 cm) high. Terra-cotta. Circa 1910.

Incised G.T. monogram. No Doulton mark.

Inscribed "G. Tinworth".

A similar plaque is illustrated in the Royal Doulton Exhibition catalogue; Sydney, 1979; page 26, L. 17.

Colour Plates

PLATE 1: Vase (before 1872) *13½" (35.6 cm) high*

PLATE 2: Jug (before 1872) *10" (24.5 cm) high*

PLATE 3A: *(left)* Vase (before 1872) *7¾" (19.4 cm) high*
PLATE 3B: *(right)* Jug (before 1872) *10½" (26.4 cm) high*

89

PLATE 4: Vase (before 1872) *10½" (26.4 cm) high*

PLATE 5: Jug (before 1872) *12¼" (31.4 cm) high*

PLATE 6: Vase (before 1872) 9½" (24.5 cm) high

PLATE 7: Jug (before 1872) 10½" (26.4 cm) high

PLATE 8: Vase (dated 1875) *12" (30.4 cm) high*

PLATE 9 : Vase (dated 1875) *10½" (26.4 cm) high*

PLATE 10: Vase (dated 1875) *12¾" (32.4 cm) high*

PLATE 11 : Vase (dated 1875) *9½" (24.5 cm) high*

PLATE 12 : Vase (dated 1875) *8½" (20.9 cm) high*

PLATE 13: Vase (dated 1877) *18" (45.5 cm) high*

PLATE 14: Vase (dated 1878)
9¾" (24.7 cm) high

PLATE 16 : Vase (dated 1877)
13¾" (34.8 cm) high

PLATE 15 : Vase (dated 1877)
10⅛" (25.8 cm) high

PLATE 17 : Vase (dated 1876)
9½" (24.2 cm) high

PLATE 18: Vase (dated 1876)
9½" (24.2 cm) high

PLATE 19 : Lemonade Jug (dated 1878) *17¼" (43.7 cm) high*

PLATE 20 : Lemonade Jug (dated 1878) *9¾" (24.7 cm) high*

PLATE 21 : Lemonade Jug (dated 1877) *13" (33.6 cm) high*

PLATE 22 : Lemonade Jug (dated 1876) *10½" (26.7 cm) high*

PLATE 23 : Lemonade Jug (dated 1875) *11¾" (29.9 cm) high*

PLATE 24 : Lemonade Jug (dated 1877) *9½" (24.3 cm) high*

PLATE 25 : Lemonade Jug (dated 1879) *9½" (24.4 cm) high*

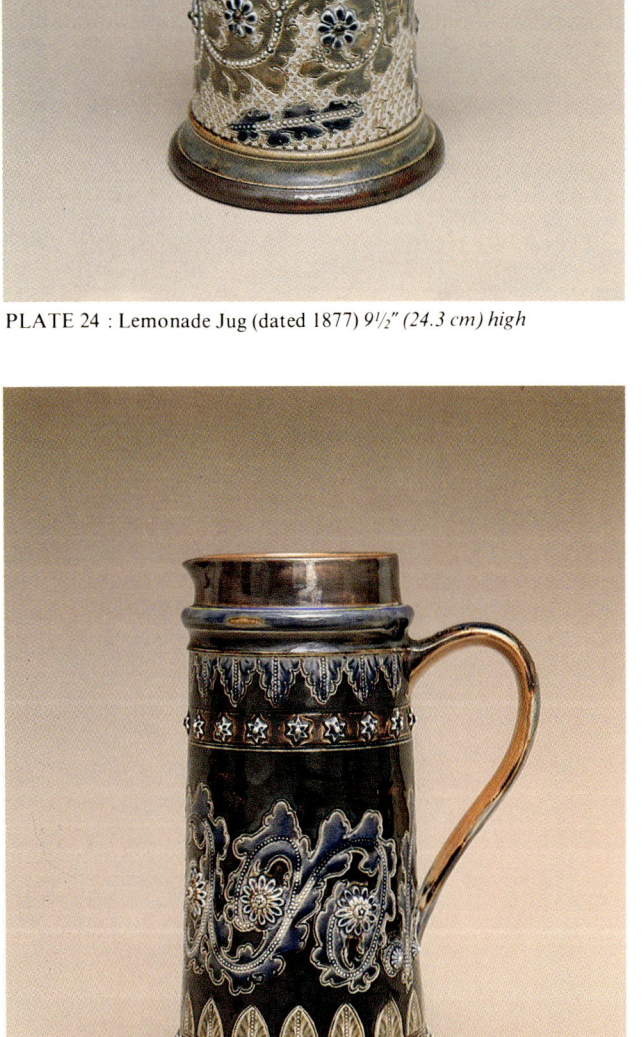
PLATE 26 : Lemonade Jug (dated 1874) *11¼" (28.7 cm) high*

PLATE 27 : Lemonade Jug and beaker (dated 1879)
9¾" (24.5 cm) & 5¼" (13.5 cm) high

PLATE 28: Vase (dated 1880) *14" (36.3 cm) high*

PLATE 29: Jug (dated 1877) *11" (28.0 cm) high*

PLATE 30: Vase (c. 1885) *20" (50.2 cm) high*

PLATE 31 : Vase (dated 1875) *8¾" (22.6 cm) high*

PLATE 32 : Vase (dated 1878) *12¼" (30.8 cm) high*

PLATE 33 : Vase (dated 1875) *10" (25.5 cm) high*

PLATE 34 : Vase (dated 1882) *12" (31.4 cm) high*

PLATE 35 : Cheese Board Cover (dated 1879) *9" (22.9 cm) high*

PLATE 36 : Commemorative Vase (c. 1887) *9¼" (23.7 cm) high*

PLATE 37: Inkwell (dated 1875) 4½" (11.4 cm) high

PLATE 38: Inkwell (dated 1877) 4½" (11.4 cm) high

PLATE 39: Candle holder (dated 1876) 8" (20.3 cm) high

PLATE 40: Candle holder (dated 1875) 6½" (15.8 cm) high

PLATE 41: Salt Cellar (c. 1875) 4" (10.1 cm) high

PLATE 42: Money box (c. 1875) 7¼" (18.4 cm) high

PLATE 43 : Vase (dated 1882) *17½" (44.4 cm) high*

PLATE 44 : Jardiniere (dated 1882) 7¾" (19.7 cm) high

PLATE 45 : Jardiniere (dated 1881) 7" (18 cm) high

PLATE 46 : Bowl (dated (1881) 5" (12.6 cm) high

PLATE 47: Plate (dated 1881) 7" (18 cm) across

PLATE 48 : Jardiniere (dated 1882) 6½" (16.5 cm) high

PLATE 49 : Vase (after 1902) *13" (33.1 cm) high*

PLATE 50 A: *(left)* Vase (after 1891) *10¾" (27.3 cm) high.* B: *(center)* Vase (c. 1900) *12¾" (32.4 cm) high.* C: *(right)* Vase (after 1902) *11" (27.9 cm) high.*

PLATE 51 A: *(left)* Vase (after 1902) *8¼" (21 cm) high.* B: *(center)* Vase (dated 1903) *12" (30.4 cm) high.* C: *(right)* Vase (after 1891) *9¼" (23.7 cm) high.*

PLATE 52 : History of England Vase
(dated 1892) *51½" (131 cm) high*

PLATE 53: History of England Vase (detail)

PLATE 54: History of England Vase (detail)

PLATE 55: History of England Vase (detail)

PLATE 56 : The Servant of Abraham (dated 1888)
20½" (52 cm) wide 13" (33 cm) high

PLATE 57: Jacob parting with Benjamin (circa 1880)
31½" (80 cm) wide by 11¾" (29.8 cm) high

PLATE: 58 : The Sons of Cydippe (dated 1884) *60" (152.5 cm) wide, 30" (76.2 cm) high*

PLATE 59: The Sons of Cydippe (detail)

PLATE 60 : The Sons of Cydippe (detail)

PLATE 61: Salome demanding the head of John the Baptist (undated) *12" (30.4 cm) wide x 5½" (14 cm) high*

PLATE 62: The Slaying of the Innocents (undated) *12" (30.4 cm) wide x 5½" (14 cm) high*

PLATE 63: The Entombment (undated) *12" (30.4 cm) wide x 5½" (14 cm) high*

PLATE 64: A Word to the Shepherds (undated) *12" (30.4 cm) wide x 5½" (14 cm) high*

PLATE 65: "The Wise and the Foolish" (c. 1871) 8¼" (21 cm) wide x 3¾" (9.5 cm) high

PLATE 66: The casting out of the money lenders (c. 1871) 8¼" (21 cm) wide x 4" (10.2 cm) high

PLATE 67: "I will draw water for the camels also" (c. 1877) 6" (15.2 cm) diameter

PLATE 68: "David would not drink of it. . ." (c. 1877) 6" (15.2 cm) diameter

115

PLATE 69: The Garden of Eden (c. 1877) *12" (30.4 cm) wide x 9" (22.9 cm) high*

PLATE 70: The Selling of Joseph (c. 1877)
12" (30.4 cm) wide x 9" (22.9 cm) high

PLATE 71: Noah and his Family (c. 1877)
12" (30.4 cm) wide x 9" (22.9 cm) high

PLATE 72: The Prodigal Son (c. 1877)
12" (30.4 cm) wide x 9" (22.9 cm) high

PLATE 73: Jesus walking on the sea (c. 1877)
12" (30.4 cm) wide x 9" (22.9 cm) high

PLATE 74: Naaman's visit to Elisha (c. 1877)
12" (30.4 cm) wide x 9" (22.9 cm) high

PLATE 75: The lost piece of silver (c. 1877)
12" (30.4 cm) wide x 9" (22.9 cm) high

PLATE 76: Jonah cast from the ship (c. 1877) *12" (30.4 cm) wide x 9" (22.9 cm) high*

PLATE 77: The Song of Miriam (c. 1877) *12" (30.4 cm) wide x 9" (22.9 cm) high*

PLATE 78: The fall of Jericho (c. 1877)
12" (30.4 cm) wide x 9" (22.9 cm) high

PLATE 79: Choosing Saul (c. 1877)
12" (30.4 cm) wide x 9" (22.9 cm) high

PLATE 80: The Good Samaritan (c. 1877)
12" (30.4 cm) wide x 9" (22.9 cm) high

PLATE 81: The Brazen Serpent (c. 1877)
12" (30.4 cm) wide x 9" (22.9 cm) high

PLATE 82: Elijah and the prophets of Baal (c. 1877)
12" (30.4 cm) wide x 9" (22.9 cm) high

PLATE 83: Raising of Jairus' Daughter (c. 1877)
12" (30.4 cm) wide x 9" (22.9 cm) high

PLATE 84: Abraham and Isaac (c. 1877) *12" (30.4 cm) wide x 9" (22.9 cm) high*

PLATE 85: David and Goliath (c. 1877) *12" (30.4 cm) wide x 9" (22.9 cm) high*

PLATE 86: Fables Clockcase (dated 1883)
11¾" (29.8 cm) wide x 10¼" (26 cm) high

PLATE 87: Fables Clockcase (detail)

PLATE 88: Menagerie Clockcase (detail) *left side*

PLATE 89: Menagerie Clockcase (detail) *right side*

PLATE 90: Menagerie Clockcase (detail)

PLATE 91: Menagerie Clockcase (c. 1885) *9½" (24.2 cm) wide x 9½" (24.2 cm) high*

PLATE 92: Menu holder: Musicians (c.1885)
3½" (8.8 cm) high

PLATE 93: Menu holder: "Organ Grinder" (c. 1885)
3¼" (8.2 cm) high

PLATE 94: Menu holder: "The Conjurors" (undated)
3½" (8.8 cm) high

PLATE 95: Menu holder: "Organ Grinder" (dated 1885)
3¾" (9.5 cm) high

PLATE 96: Menu holder: "The Conjurors" (dated 1885)
3½" (8.8 cm) high

PLATE 97: Menu holder: "Potter" (c. 1885)
3¾" (9.5 cm) high

PLATE 98: Menu holder: "Cornet Blowers" (c. 1885)
3½" (8.8 cm) high

PLATE 99: Menu holder: "Quack Doctor" (c. 1885)
4" (10.2 cm) high

PLATE 100: Menu holder: "Musicians" (dated 1886)
3½" (8.8 cm) high

PLATE 101: Menu Holder: "The Wheelwright" (dated 1886)
3¾" (9.5 cm) high

PLATE 102: Menu holder: "The Sculptor" (dated 1886)
4" (10.2 cm) high

PLATE 103: Menu holder: "Painting" (c. 1885)
3½" (8.8 cm) high

PLATE 104: Mouse Group "The Cockneys at Brighton" (dated 1886) 4" (10.2 cm) high

PLATE 105: Tile: "Photography" (undated) 6" (15.2 cm) square

PLATE 106: Mouse Group "The Drunkards" (c. 1885) 3¼" (8.3 cm) high

PLATE 107: Frog and Mouse group "The Steeplechase" (undated) 4½" (11.5 cm) high

PLATE 108: Mouse group "Tea-time Scandal" (c. 1888) 4" (10.2 cm) high

PLATE 109: Mouse flute player (dated 1884) 3½" (8.8 cm) high

PLATE 110: Mouse on currant bun (dated 1884) 3" (7.6 cm) high

PLATE 111: Mouse cornet player (dated 1886) 3⅛" (8 cm) high

PLATE 112:
Mouse group "Playgoers"
(after 1891) 5½" (14 cm) high

PLATE 113: Mouse group "Niggers" (undated)
3¾" (9.5 cm) high

PLATE 114: "The Pillars of Wealth and Poverty Between" (undated)
4¼" (10.8 cm) high

PLATE 115: Mouse group "Waits" (undated) 5¼" (13.3 cm) high

PLATE 116: Fob watch holder (undated)
4½" (11.5 cm) high

PLATE 117: Mouse chess set (c. 1885): The Reds

PLATE 118: Mouse chess set: A game in progress

PLATE 119: Mouse chess set: The Blacks

PLATE 120: Frog group: Going to the Derby (c. 1885) *4" (10.2 cm) high*

PLATE 121: Frog group: Returning from the Derby (c. 1885) *4" (10.2 cm) high*

PLATE 122: Frog group: "Jack in the Green" (c. 1885) 5¼" (13.3 cm) high

PLATE 123: Frog group: "Bicyclist" (c. 1885) 4½" (11.5 cm) high

PLATE 124: Frog group: "The Public Library's Act" (c. 1884) 5¼" (13.3 cm) high

PLATE 125: Frog group: "The Football Scrimmage" (c. 1885) 5" (12.7 cm) high

PLATE 126: Frog group: "The Football Scrimmage" (c. 1885) 5" (12.7 cm) high (reverse)

PLATE 127: Animal group: "Safe Travelling" (c. 1885) 6¾" (17.2 cm) high

PLATE 128: Fable group: "The Monkey"
(c. 1882) 4" (10.2 cm) high

PLATE 129: "The Waning of the Honeymoon"
(dated 1880) 4¾" (12.1 cm) high

PLATE 130: Fable group: "The Ox and The Frogs" (dated 1881) 7" (17.8 cm) wide x 3" (7.6 cm) high

PLATE 131: Monkey group: "A United Family" (after 1891) 4¾" (12.1 cm) high

PLATE 132: Fable group: "Monkey, Cats and Cheese" (dated 1882) 6" (15.2 cm) high

PLATE 133: Plaque: Donkeys (c. 1875) 5½" (14 cm) wide x 7½" (19 cm) high

PLATE 134: Candlesticks with boy soldiers (undated) *12¾" (32.4 cm) high*

PLATE 135: Seated Youth (undated) *12¾" (32.4 cm) high*

PLATE 136: Seated Youth (undated) *12¾" (32.4 cm) high*

PLATE 137: The Swimming Bath (undated) *11½" (29.2 cm) wide x 3¾" (9.5 cm) high*

PLATE 138: *(left side)* The Swimming Bath (detail)

PLATE 139: *(right side)* The Swimming Bath (detail)

PLATE 140:
Circular plaque with seated woman
(undated) 9½" (24.1 cm) diameter

PLATE 141A: *(left)* Salt cellar: A boy drummer (c. 1885) 3½" (9 cm) high
PLATE 141B: *(right)* Salt cellar: "Fowl" (c. 1885) 4" (10.2 cm) high

PLATE 142: Spill vase: boy with two vases (c. 1885) 5¼" (13.3 cm) high

PLATE 143: "The Telephone: Good News"
(c. 1885) 4½" (11.5 cm) high

141

PLATE 144: Flower holder:
Cherubs riding seahorses (dated 1878)
4¾" (12 cm) high

PLATE 145: Clockcase: Tennis players *10" (25.4 cm) high*

PLATE 146: A Band of Merry Musicians

PLATE 147: Musician: Viola player (after 1892)
4¾" (12 cm) high

PLATE 148: Jester: Mandolin player (undated) *7" (15.2 cm) high*

PLATE 149: Musician: Banjo player (undated)
4½" (11.4 cm) high

PLATE 150: The Jester (c. 1900) 12½" (31.7 cm) high

PLATE 151: The boy jester (undated) 5" (12.7 cm) high

144

PLATE 152: Head of Man (c. 1890) *18" (45.4 cm) high*

PLATE 153: Girl with tambourine (undated) *9" (22.9 cm) high*

PLATE 154: Tambourine player (undated) *15" (38.1 cm) high*

PLATE 155: Spill vase: "5 miles to London" (c. 1885) 9" (22.8 cm) high

PLATE 156: Plaque: Spring (undated)
6½" (16.5 cm) wide x 12¾" (32.4 cm) high

PLATE 157: Plaque: Summer (undated)
6½" (16.5 cm) wide x 12¾" (32.4 cm) high

PLATE 158 Plaque: Autumn (undated)
6½" (16.5 cm) wide x 12¾" (32.4 cm) high

PLATE 159 Plaque: Winter (undated)
6½" (16.5 cm) wide x 12¾" (32.4 cm) high

PLATE 160 A: *(left)* Plaque: "Seed Time" (c. 1876)   4¼" (10.8 cm) wide x 8½" (21.6 cm) high
PLATE 160 B: *(right)* Plaque: "Summer Time" (c. 1876)   4¼" (10.8 cm) wide x 8½" (21.6 cm) high

PLATE 161 A: *(left)* Plaque: "Harvest Time" (c. 1876)   4¼" (10.8 cm) wide x 8½" (21.6 cm) high
PLATE 161 B: *(right)* Plaque: "Winter Time" (c. 1876)   4¼" (10.8 cm) wide x 8½" (21.6 cm) high

PLATE 162: "The Drunken Husband" (c. 1880) *5¼" (13.3 cm) high*

PLATE 163: "The Drunken Husband" (detail)

PLATE 164: The Carpenters Bag (after 1891) 3½" (9 cm) high

Chronology of Principal Works by George Tinworth

Compiled by Desmond Eyles

Chronology

The following catalogue of George Tinworth's panels and other sculpture is based on Doulton records, press notices and information gathered over many years from museum authorities, antique dealers, collectors, former Doulton colleagues of Tinworth, and others interested in the work of this remarkable artist. For the period before 1882, I am much indebted to the catalogue of the Fine Arts Society exhibition of 1883, compiled by Edmund (later Sir Edmund) Gosse.

The list, extensive as it is, cannot claim to be complete — for additional examples of Tinworth's work come to light almost every year. Information about any items not included here will, therefore, be welcomed by the publishers, with a view to possible inclusion in any future edition or supplement.

Much more information has been found about some pieces than about others; the amount of space given to any particular work is thus not necessarily related to its importance. The measurements of some panels are not recorded; those of others show slight differences between one record and another — probably due to whether or not the frames were included. When the exact date of production is not known, the estimated period is given. In such cases the work is listed under the *later* of the two dates shown.

Copies of some smaller panels were reproduced from moulds. Tinworth insisted on inspecting all such copies in the clay state before firing and sometimes made slight or even substantial alterations. Copies of the larger panels were rarely made.

Tinworth's humorous animal studies and other creations in the genre are described in detail in the Harriman-Judd Ceramic Collection catalogue.

During his almost 50 years at Lambeth, Tinworth and his assistants also decorated many thousands of vases, jugs, bowls, tankards, candlesticks and similar domestic wares. It is impossible to catalogue these, but examples of the various decorative surface treatments and shapes of such pieces are illustrated and fully described in the catalogue.

Abbreviations

V & A Museum for the Victoria & Albert Museum, Cromwell Road, London, SW7.

Cuming Museum for the Cuming Museum, Walworth Road, London, SE17.

Sydney Museum for the Museum of Applied Arts and Sciences, Sydney, New South Wales, Australia.

Dennis I for the catalogue of an exhibition of Doulton Stoneware and Terracotta 1870-1925, Part One, held in London in 1971 by Richard Dennis.

Dennis II for the catalogue of an exhibition of Doulton Pottery from the Lambeth and Burslem Studios 1873-1939, Part Two, held in London in 1975 by Richard Dennis.

Minet Library for the Woolley Collection in the Minet Library, Knatchbull Road, London SE5.

Unless otherwise stated all the places mentioned in this catalogue are in England.

1861

1861: HANDEL — a bust carved in Portland Stone. It was this which Tinworth showed to Mr. Sparkes on his first visit to the Lambeth School of Art; on the strength of it he was admitted as a student.

1862

1862: THE MOCKING OF CHRIST — with this terracotta panel (for which Tinworth's brother, Tom, sat as a model) the artist won a £2 prize at the Lambeth School of Art.

A cast of the panel, 27″ (68.6 cm) wide x 16″ (40.5)cm high, is in the Cuming Museum.

1864

1864: HERCULES — a figure modelled from a copy of the antique original under the direction of Mr. Sparkes. This was awarded a Bronze Medal at the Lambeth School of Art and gained Tinworth entrance to the Antique School of the Royal Academy as a probationer.

1864: JASON — a figure with which Tinworth obtained a seven years' studentship at the Royal Academy.

1864: During this year Tinworth assisted Percival Ball (one of the Lambeth Art School's most promising students who later became a well-known sculptor in Florence) in modelling several over-life-sized heads for the facade of an extension to Doulton's Lambeth Pottery. Designed by John Sparkes, they portrayed Wedgwood, Böttger, Palissy and other potters — the head of each potter alternating with a female head symbolising the country in which he had worked.

1865

1865: THE DYING GLADIATOR — a figure which won for Tinworth the Second Silver Medal in the Antique School of the Royal Academy.

1865: PARIS — a figure modelled by Tinworth as a 24 hour life study.

1866

1866: PEACE AND WRATH IN LOW LIFE — Tinworth's work was exhibited for the first time at the Royal Academy with this group of small figures in plaster. Based directly on the sculptor's first-hand observation of a slum environment in Walworth, it portrayed two little boys having a fight, two little girls trying to separate them, and a mongrel dog barking in the foreground.

After having been exhibited again in Paris in 1867, the group was unfortunately destroyed.

A small salt-glaze stoneware panel, 8½″ (21.5 cm) wide x 4″ (10 cm) high, entitled A STREET SCENE IN WALWORTH, is in the Cuming Museum. Also based on direct experience, it was probably conceived about the same time, although it may not have been made until some years later.

1867

1867: STUDY FROM LIFE — a 30 hour study with which Tinworth won the First Silver Medal at the Royal Academy. By this time the sculptor had been found work at Doulton's Lambeth Pottery at the remuneration of £1.50 a week.

1868

1868: JOHN DOULTON — a large terracotta bust of the founder of the Doulton Potteries. Exhibited in this year at the Royal Academy, it was not, in the opinion of Edmund Gosse, really "a work of merit".

In connection with this bust, Tinworth related the following in his "Life Story": "(John Doulton) brought Mr. Henry Doulton and his granddaughter, Miss Kitty Doulton, to see it. She was about fourteen then. The old gentleman nudged me to take the cloth off, as it was covered over, while he got her to look the other way . . . he told her to look and asked 'Who is that, my dear?' and she said: 'Why! you grandpa!' Then he kissed her." Soon after this, Tinworth also did busts of Kitty and her sister, Lilian.

1868: A series of terracotta medallions based upon portraits on Greek and Sicilian coins —

> ALEXANDER THE GREAT, 45″ (114 cm) diam.
> PROSERPINA, 45″ (114 cm) diam.
> HERCULES, 43″ (109 cm) diam.
> MEDUSA, 46″ (117 cm) diam.
> ARETHUSA, 26½″ (67 cm) diam.
> TWO FEMALE HEADS, 25½″ (64 cm) diam.

These large medallions proved popular and were reproduced from moulds over many years. They were still featured in a Doulton catalogue dated 1897. It was these medallions, especially the one of Hercules wearing a lion's head as a hood, which, according to Edmund Gosse, first attracted the attention of John Ruskin to the young artist whom he afterwards so greatly encouraged by his continuing interest in his work (See figure 5).

1869

1869: HERCULES AND ANTAEUS — a figure group entered unsuccessfully by Tinworth for the Royal Academy Gold Medal competition.

1869: Large terracotta FOUNTAIN — modelled from a design by John Sparkes, it was covered with fanciful ornament and surmounted by the figure of a man holding a cross. It was donated by Sir Henry Doulton to Kennington Park in south-east London and stood there for many years. Only the central shaft now remains; this features a sculpture by Tinworth entitled "The Pilgrimage of Life".

1870

1870: THE "AMAZON" or "AMAZONIAN" VASE — this is the name given to a spectacular vase, c. 70″ (178 cm) high, which Tinworth designed for the 1871 International Exhibition at South Kensington, London. Decorated with a frieze of fighting Amazons, it had handles, in the shape of wild horses, springing out from the body of the vase. Tinworth conceived the idea for this vase, it is thought, after seeing, in the British Museum, part of a frieze from the temple of Apollo at Bassae.

1870: STUDY FROM LIFE — a terracotta panel, 10½″ (26.5 cm) wide x 20″ (51 cm) high, executed at the Royal Academy. No other details recorded.

1871

1871: Twelve inlaid relief panels in salt-glaze stoneware — part of an ebonised and gilded wood cabinet. Eight of the panels illustrate the following parables: THE TEN VIRGINS; THE LABOURERS IN THE VINEYARD; THE ONE WHO SOWED TARES; THE PRODIGAL SON; THE WICKED HUBANDMEN; THE WICKED SERVANT; THE FEAST TO THE POOR; THE NET. The other four depict: ZACCHEUS; THE CRUCIFIXION; OVERTURNING THE TABLES OF THE MONEY-CHANGERS; THE INSTITUTION OF THE PASSOVER.

Shown in the 1872 London International Exhibition, the cabinet was bought by the South Kensington (now the Victoria and Albert) Museum, where it may still be seen (See figure 6).

(See Plates 65 and 66 for two small panels which appear closely related to two of the above.)

1871: Salt cellar in salt-glaze stoneware modelled with four scenes in high relief relating to the betrayal and crucifixion of Jesus, each scene comprising three figures: (1) SATAN PREPARETH JUDAS TO BETRAY HIM (Judas conspiring with two priests); (2) PETER'S DENIAL (Peter talking to the maidservant and the Roman soldier); (3) AND THE SOLDIERS PLAITED A CROWN OF THORNS (three soldiers, one of whom is holding the wreath of thorns); (4) THEY CAST LOTS FOR HIS GARMENTS (three soldiers throwing dice).

A characteristic Tinworth touch is one of the soldiers plaiting the wreath who has pricked his finger and is holding it to his lips.

The salt-cellar is inscribed at the base with the artist's own name and that of Mr. Henry Doulton, for whom it was made, also the date 1871. Inscribed around the bowl are the words from Matthew V, 13: "Ye are the salt of the earth but if the salt have lost his savour, wherewith shall it be salted?" The scourge, the hammer and the nails are indicated as symbols of the Crucifixion.

1871: PETER IN PRISON — a salt-glaze stoneware panel, 4" (10.2 cm) square, showing the apostle being aroused by an angel while two soldiers are still asleep on the floor of the cell.

There is another salt-glaze stoneware panel illustrating the same subject, but 4½" (11.5 cm) x 3½" (9.0 cm), in the Sydney Museum.

1873

1873: Four medallions in salt-glaze stoneware symbolising: FAITH, HOPE, CHARITY and RESIGNATION.

Designed for a monument in Belfast, Ireland; details of which are not recorded.

1873: AQUARIUS — a large medallion in salt-glaze stoneware designed as part of a fountain; other details not recorded.

1873: Three terracotta panels, c. 12" (30.5 cm) wide x 5½" (14 cm) high, designed as sketches for the three large panels: GETHSEMANE, THE FOOT OF THE CROSS and THE DESCENT FROM THE CROSS completed the following year.

These small panels are now in the Methodist Church, Trentham, Staffs.

1874

1871-1874: A series of salt-glaze stoneware panels closely resembling those in the 1871 cabinet, c. 8¼″ (21 cm) wide x 4″ (10 cm) high, depicting: BALAAM MEETING THE ANGEL; THE CASTING OUT OF THE MONEY-LENDERS; THE WISE AND THE FOOLISH; ZACCHAEUS; DAVID'S LAW; THE PEACEABLE KINGDOM OF CHRIST; THE GARDEN OF EDEN; THE PARABLE OF THE SOWER.

See Plates 65 and 66 and Dennis I, 662, for similar panels to some of the above.

1874: Three terracotta panels, c. 56″ (142 cm) wide x 30″ (75 cm) high, entitled: GETHSEMANE, THE FOOT OF THE CROSS, and THE DESCENT FROM THE CROSS.

These panels were exhibited at the Royal Academy in 1874 and were bought by the Museum of Science and Art in Edinburgh, Scotland.

Some twenty years after completing THE DESCENT FROM THE CROSS, Tinworth mentioned to a visitor to his studio why he had shown the soldiers using wedges, crow-bars and mallets to release the nails: "My father". he said, "always made me split disused wood to get out the nails and save them up."

1875: Eight terracotta panels, each c. 12″ (30.5 cm) wide x 5½″ (14 cm) high, exhibited at the Royal Academy. They illustrated the following subjects: THE BROW OF THE HILL; THE ENTRY INTO JERUSALEM; THE ADORATION OF THE MAGI; TOUCHING THE HEM OF OUR LORD'S GARMENT; WAITING FOR THE HEAD OF JOHN THE BAPTIST (also described as THE DAUGHTER OF HERODIAS); PETER'S DENIAL; CHRIST BLESSING THE LITTLE CHILDREN; THE RELEASE OF BARABBAS (also known as THE JUDGEMENT OF PILATE).

These were panels which evoked the generous tribute from John Ruskin quoted in Chapter II of the Life.

1875

1875: THE TIMES OF SOLOMON — 28 small salt-glaze stoneware alto-relievo panel studies, profusely inscribed with appropriate texts, illustrating from incidents in the Bible the "times" referred to in Ecclesiastes iii, 1-8. These were shown at the Fine Art Society Exhibition of 1883, arranged in two panels, and were then described as being "designed for the ornament of a vase". They were again exhibited at the Cuming Museum in December 1910.

The subjects chosen by Tinworth to illustrate the various "times" show his intimate knowledge of the Bible and, some of them, such as 13, 16, 18, 22 and 23, his flashes of humour:

(1) A TIME TO BE BORN (depicting the Virgin and Child);
(2) A TIME TO DIE (the death of Samson);
(3) A TIME TO PLANT (Noah planting a vineyard);
(4) A TIME TO PLUCK UP THAT WHICH IS PLANTED (the disciples plucking the ears of corn);
(5) A TIME TO KILL (Samson slaying the lion);
(6) A TIME TO HEAL (the healing by Jesus of "the man with an unclean spirit");

(7) A TIME TO BREAK DOWN (Gideon breaking down the altar of Baal);
(8) A TIME TO BUILD UP (Building the walls of Jerusalem);
(9) A TIME TO WEEP (the repentance of St. Peter);
(10) A TIME TO LAUGH (Sarah nursing Isaac);
(11) A TIME TO MOURN (Naomi parting with Ruth and Orpah, her daughters-in-law);
(12) A TIME TO DANCE (Miriam at the Red Sea);
(13) A TIME TO CAST AWAY STONES (David before Goliath);
(14) A TIME TO GATHER STONES TOGETHER (the scene at the Jordan referred to in Joshuah iv, 3);
(15) A TIME TO EMBRACE (the raising of the Shunamite's son by Elisha);
(16) A TIME TO REFRAIN FROM EMBRACING (Joseph fleeing from Potiphar's wife who had tempted him to adultery);
(17) A TIME TO GET (Delilah counting the money brought to her by the lords of the Philistines);
(18) A TIME TO LOSE (Samson finding his hair gone after being enticed by Delilah);
(19) A TIME TO KEEP (One of David's three mighty men with the bottle of water — an incident described in 2 Samuel, xxiii);
(20) A TIME TO CAST AWAY (Judas casting down the pieces of silver paid to him for the betrayal of Jesus);
(21) A TIME TO REND (Job rending his garment after experiencing misfortune);
(22) A TIME TO SEW (Adam sewing fig leaves together to conceal his nakedness);
(23) A TIME TO KEEP SILENCE (Miriam watching Moses in the ark of bulrushes);
(24) A TIME TO SPEAK (Queen Esther before Ahasuerus, as described in Esther V);
(25) A TIME TO LOVE (Jesus turning to look at Peter who had thrice denied him);
(26) A TIME TO HATE (King Ahasuerus in his wrath looking upon Haman (Esther vii);
(27) A TIME OF WAR. (David with the head of Goliath);
(28) A TIME OF PEACE (Adam in the Garden of Eden before the fall),

1875: A salt-glaze stoneware sketch model for the pulpit described below.

1875: A pulpit in red and buff terracotta and salt-glaze stoneware, exhibited at the Centennial Exhibition, Philadelphia in 1876, and later presented to the Smithsonian Institute, Washington D.C.

The pulpit, which measured c. 101½" (258 cm) wide, 137" (348 cm) long and 104½" (265.5 cm) high, had subsequently to be dismantled to make room for other exhibits and only four terracotta groups, each portraying three figures, remain — some badly damaged during the dismantling.

There were originally five groups representing: (1) THE PRESENTATION OF THE INFANT SAVIOUR IN THE TEMPLE; (2) GETHSEMANE; (3) CHRIST CROWNED WITH THORNS: (4) THE JOURNEY TO EMMAUS; (5) THE THREE MARYS AT THE RESURRECTION.

On the door of the pulpit, Tinworth had depicted a bird's nest, recalling the passage in St. Luke ix, 58: "The birds of the air have nests, but the Son of Man hath not where to lay his head." This, he told a clergyman who visited his studio before the pulpit went to America, was to remind the bishops and canons, perched in pulpits in all their finery, of the contrast between them and the founder of Christianity. Years afterwards, the same clergyman, Dr. Benson, by then Archbishop of Canterbury, visited Tinworth's studio for the second time and reminded the sculptor of his "good advice".

1875: A sketch model for the font described below.

1875: A font in terracotta and salt-glaze stoneware, exhibited at the Centennial Exhibition in 1876, and — like the pulpit already described — presented to the Smithsonian Institution. The font also was subsequently demolished, and only the eight salt-glaze stoneware panels which originally formed part of it still remain.

The panels, each c. 12¼" (31 cm) wide x 5½" (14 cm) high, all portray scenes relating to children mentioned in the Bible: (1) THE ADORATION OF THE SHEPHERDS; (2) THE VISIT OF THE MAGI; (3) THE MASSACRE OF THE INNOCENTS; (4) CHRIST BLESSING LITTLE CHILDREN; (5) THE LESSON OF HUMILITY; (6) THE FINDING OF MOSES; (7) THE JUDGMENT OF SOLOMON; (8) THE SHUNAMITE'S SON.

1875: A reproduction in terracotta, for the Philadephia Exhibition, of John Bell's marble group symbolising AMERICA, part of the Albert Memorial in Kensington Gardens, London. It consisted of five figures, each about 120" (304 cm) high, with a buffalo in the middle.

Tinworth collaborated with Bell in the reproduction of this colossal group which was fired without a flaw or crack. Each figure was moulded separately and the number of joins was fewer than in the marble original. The result, according to Bell, was one of the most remarkable feats that any English potter had ever accomplished.

1875: A large salt-glaze stoneware jug with small applied panels depicting biblical scenes (See figure 7).

1876

1876: Four terracotta panels, each c. 18" (45.7 cm) x 11" (28 cm), exhibited at the Royal Academy Exhibition of that year, depicting: (1) THE STABLE, also known as THE ADORATION OF THE SHEPHERDS; (2) THE REMORSE OF JUDAS; (3) DAVID WITH THE HEAD OF GOLIATH; (4) PAUL AND BARNABAS AT LYSTRA. As usual in many of Tinworth-religious panels, there are numerous references to scriptural texts.

These panels attracted the attention of the then well-known architect, Mr. G.E. Street, R.A. Street and Ruskin and visited Tinworth several times in his studio, giving him encouragement and advice, and Street later obtained for him important commissions — especially for a reredos for York Minster and a series of panels for the Royal Military Chapel (The Guards' Chapel) in Birdcage Walk, London.

Panel (3), or a similar one, is now in the Sydney Museum.

1876: THE FOOTBALL SCRIMMAGE — a terracotta figure group in the round, exhibited at the Royal Academy the following year, and again at the Paris Exhibition of 1878.

1876: THE FOUR SEASONS — a set of four small salt-glaze stoneware panels, bought by Lord Ronald Gower.

These closely resemble Plates 160A, 160B, 161A, 161B.

1876: A reproduction, c. 126" (320 cm) high, of the statue of DIANA WITH THE STAG in the Louvre in Paris.

Until it was destroyed during World War II, this statue stood on the left of the entrance to the Doulton Showrooms on the Albert Embankment. London. On the right hand side was a colossal piece of salt-glaze stoneware chemical apparatus; the two exhibits symbolised Doulton's two main interests in the field of ceramics — *Art* and *Industry*.

Another copy of the statue was made for the Philadelphia Exhibition.

Fig. 22. Terra-cotta panel: The Doulton Artists, 1876.

1876: THE DOULTON ARTISTS — a semi-circular terracotta panel which may still be seen over the corner entrance to the former Doulton offices in High Street, Lambeth. It depicts some of the artists at the Lambeth Studios at that time, including Hannah Barlow with one of her pet cats under her chair, and probably Frank A. Butler, Arthur B. Barlow and Tinworth himself. Henry Doulton is in the centre, and in the background a load of pots is being taken to the kiln, carried on a board on the kilnsman's head (See Figure 22).

1876: Terracotta sketch of the reredos described below.

1876: Terracotta reredos, c. 113″ (287 cm) wide x 60″ (152.5 cm) high, for York Minster, representing THE CRUCIFIXION.

This reredos, Tinworth's first important outside commission, is a remarkable piece of work, embracing no fewer than 36 different figures in semi-relief. From 1876 to 1937 the reredos was behind the high altar of the Minster; then, because of alterations, it had to be moved and is now on the east wall of the St. Stephen's Chapel (See Figure 9).

A very human touch, characteristic of Tinworth, is a small boy on the right sucking his finger which he has just withdrawn from the jar of vinegar. Other examples of Tinworth's vivid imagination are the old Pharisee looking rather cynically at Mary; a young soldier putting his hand into the Saviour's wound; a negro looking up towards Jesus; and the introduction of Barabbas who has earlier been released in preference to Jesus and is now among the mockers.

Edmund Gosse thought that the solemn scene would have been more effective in bas-relief, "but", he said, "Mr. Tinworth does not think so, and we must not measure him too rigidly by our own conventional standards."

1877

1877: THE WHEELWRIGHT'S SHOP — a terracotta panel, 8″ (20.3 cm) square, modelled in high relief, illustrating an actual incident in the sculptor's life.

Tinworth, as a young man, is seen carving a head in his father's workshop, while his mother looks on, and a boy is posted at the door so as to warn Tinworth immediately when his father (who did not approve of his son "carving graven images") comes in sight.

It seems that several copies of this panel, some with slight variations, were made and "retouched" in the clay state by Tinworth. Smaller versions only 6″ (15.2 cm) square are also extant.

Examples of the larger panel are in the Doulton collection at Stoke-on-Trent; Lambeth Town Hall, London; and the Willett Collection in Brighton Art Gallery (See Figure 3).

One version of this panel is recorded as having been introduced into the base of the fountain next described.

1877: Fountain and base in salt-glaze stoneware, c. 216″ (548 cm) high overall, exhibited at the Paris Exhibition in 1878 and again at the Worcestershire Exhibition in 1882.

The overall shape of the fountain is a cone fixed in a circular basin. A water channel descends in a spiral round the sides of the cone into the basin below. The retaining wall of the channel is made in sections decorated with small relief panels. These illustrate biblical events connected in some way with water and inscribed with relevant texts and references. Working from the base of the column upwards they show:

(1) JONAH ESCAPING FROM THE FISH'S BELLY;
(2) SAMSON DRINKING WATER FROM THE JAW-BONE OF AN ASS;
(3) THE DISCOVERY OF MOSES IN THE BULRUSHES;
(4) MOSES AT THE WELL, PROTECTING THE DAUGHTERS OF THE PRIEST OF MIDIAN;

(5) GIDEON SELECTING HIS SOLDIERS AT THE WATER-SIDE;
(6) ST. PAUL, AFTER HIS SHIPWRECK, ATTACKED BY A VIPER;
(7) CHRIST CHANGING WATER INTO WINE AT THE MARRIAGE OF CANA;
(8) THE HEALING OF THE IMPOTENT MAN AT THE POOL OF BETHESDA;
(9) ELIJAH, ABOUT TO OFFER SACRIFICE ON MOUNT CARMEL, TELLS THE PEOPLE TO FILL FOUR BARRELS WITH WATER;
(10) THE BAPTISM IN THE JORDAN;
(11) DAVID POURING OUT WATER FROM THE WELL AT BETHLEHEM;
(12) MIRIAM, MOSES AND AARON AT THE RED SEA;
(13) THE LEPER NAAMAN WASHING IN THE JORDAN;
(14) REBEKAH AT THE WELL;
(15) THE WOMAN OF SAMARIA AT THE WELL;
(16) THE CLEANSING OF THE LEPER UNDER THE MOSAIC LAW;
(17) ABRAHAM DISMISSING HAGAR AND ISHMAEL;
(18) ELIJAH AND THE WIDOW OF SAREPTA;
(19) ELIJAH FED BY RAVENS;
(20) MOSES AFTER STRIKING THE ROCK TO OBTAIN WATER.

The apex of the column depicts the Flood, with the people trying to escape from the deluge, while eagles hover overhead. The spaces between the panels are occupied by various animals, birds and reptiles.

The fountain, restored thanks to the efforts of the well-known authority on Doulton Wares, Richard Dennis, was shown at the Doulton exhibition held at the V & A Museum in 1979 (See Figure 11).

(See Plate 68 for a slightly different treatment of (2) relating to the incident described in 2 Samuel, xxiii.)

1877: A bowl for a font in salt-glaze stoneware, with sixteen relief panels illustrating.

(1) THE TOWER OF BABEL;
(2) CHRIST DRIVING THE MONEY-CHANGERS OUT OF THE TEMPLE;
(3) THE DEATH OF JEZEBEL;
(4) HAMAN AND MORDECAI;
(5) DAVID AND MICHAL;
(6) THE DEATH OF THE ISRAELITISH LORD;
(7) RAHAB;
(8) JOSEPH'S BRETHREN;
(9) ST. PAUL'S ESCAPE FROM DAMASCUS;
(10) LOT AND THE ANGELS;
(11) THE SIEGE OF THEBEZ;
(12) THE PASSOVER;
(13) BUILDING THE WALL OF JERUSALEM;
(14) THE TEN VIRGINS;
(15) THE MAN SICK OF THE PALSY;
(16) JEREMIAH.
Part of this font is in the V & A Museum.

1878

1878: A series of 28 semi-circular terracotta panels for the Royal Military Chapel (the Guard's Chapel) in Birdcage Walk, London, SWI.

The biblical events portrayed were:

(1) THE GARDEN OF EDEN;
(2) THE ARK;
(3) THE OFFERING OF ISAAC;
(4) THE RAGE OF ESAU;
(5) THE SELLING OF JOSEPH;
(6) THE SONG OF MIRIAM;
(7) THE BRAZEN SERPENT;
(8) JOSHUA RECEIVING RAHAB;
(9) THE FINDING OF SAUL
(10) DAVID KILLING GOLIATH OF GATH;
(11) THE SACRIFICE ON MOUNT CARMEL;
(12) THE VISIT OF NAAMAN THE LEPER TO ELISHA;
(13) DANIEL IN THE LION'S DEN;
(14) THE DEATH OF SIMON THE MACCABEEAN;
(15) THE RAISING OF LAZARUS;
(16) CHRIST AT THE HOUSE OF SIMON THE LEPER;
(17) THE ROMAN CENTURION;
(18) FINDING THE LOST PIECE OF MONEY;
(19) THE MIRACULOUS PIECE OF MONEY;
(20) THE FOOLISH VIRGINS;
(21) CHRIST RECEIVING LITTLE CHILDREN;
(22) THE HEALING OF BARTIMAEUS;
(23) THE PRODIGAL SON;
(24) CHRIST WALKING ON THE SEA;
(25) THE GOOD SAMARITAN;
(26) THE RAISING OF JAIRUS' DAUGHTER;
(270 THE LABOURERS IN THE VINEYARD;
(28) THE TURNING OF WATER INTO WINE.

Among the interesting features of these panels are the following:

THE GARDEN OF EDEN — one of the very few examples of Tinworth's portrayal of the nude. A typical Tinworth addition in DANIEL IN THE LION'S DEN is the representation of one of the lions standing on its hind legs to read an inscription on the top of the walled den: "Psa. xci". On turning up the Psalm we find the words: "Thou shalt tread upon the lion." Tinworth's interpretation of the parable FINDING THE LOST PIECE OF MONEY is vividly portrayed. The woman who finds money is bending over her garden fence to draw her neighbours' attention to her discovery — one of these looks as pleased as if she found the coin herself (See Figure 10).

The chapel was destroyed by a bomb during World War II and nearly all the panels installed there were damaged beyond repair.

1878: THE SOWING OF TARES — another semi-circular terracotta panel apparently originally intended for the Guards' Chapel, but not used (See Figure 23).

1878: THE DESCENT FROM THE CROSS — a terracotta panel exhibited at the Paris Exhibition of 1878 and erected five years later in Sandringham Church, Norfolk.

Fig. 23. *"The Sowing of Tares"*. An unused lunette illustrated in the 1883 catalogue. (*Royal Army Chaplaincy Museum,* Bagshot).

1878: HAGAR AND ISHMAEL — a terracotta panel, 6″ (15.25 cm) square, exhibited at the Royal Academy in 1878.

1879

1879: THE GARDEN OF GETHSEMANE — a small terracotta panel, one of several on this subject modelled by Tinworth at various times. He hoped one day to come back to it in a very large panel which would be his great masterpiece. He was working on this shortly before his death, but apparently never finished it.

1879: GOING TO CALVARY — a terracotta panel, c. 120″ (305 cm) wide x 48″ (122 cm) high, exhibited at the Royal Academy in 1880. It depicts Jesus turning towards the weeping daughters of Jerusalem, as recorded in Luke xxiii, 28. Pilate and his wife look on as Simon the Cyrenian is forced by soldiers to bear the cross, and Barabbas receives his friends' congratulations on his release. On the right, the two thieves are being led to execution. In the foreground women scatter lilies in the pathway of the Saviour.

Characteristic of Tinworth's imaginative interpretation of the gospel story are Barabbas shading his eyes after confinement in a dark prison, the mother of the penitent thief saying a last good-bye to him, and the centurion in charge of the crucifixion leaning forward over his horse's head to ascertain the cause of a scuffle in the crowd.

The panel was erected in Truro Cathedral, Cornwall, in 1902, where it may still be seen in the north choir aisle in a glass-fronted case. Underneath is a brass tablet bearing the inscription: "To the glory of God, from F. Walters Bond, D.L., J.P., High Sheriff of Berkshire A.D. 1900-1901, a native of Cornwall, as a thank-offering for the safe return of two sons from the war in South Africa in 1902."

Mr. Bond bought the Panel after the Royal Academy Exhibition in 1880 for 500 guineas (See Figure 24).

Fig. 24. Terra-cotta panel: *"Going to Calvary"*.

1880

1880: THE CRUCIFIXION — a terracotta panel, c. 42″ (105.5 cm) wide x 18″ (46 cm) high, designed and executed for Earl Brownlow and fixed in a reredos in Colmere Church.

1880: THE CITY OF REFUGE — a terracotta panel, c. 72″ (183 cm) wide x 30″ (75 cm) high, designed and executed for the lintel of the Baptist Church, Wraysbury, near Windsor, Berks, where it still is in very good condition. It is one of the few Tinworth panels incorporated in the outside of a building.

Tinworth sometimes stayed in Wraysbury with the family of James D. Doulton, younger brother of Henry. James was deacon and secretary of the church from 1870 to 1900. The Doulton residence, Tinworth once told a colleague, was for him "a real city of refuge".

In the United Reform Church at East Sheen, Mortlake, London, there is a smaller panel, c. 16″ (40 cm) wide x 8″ (20 cm) high, illustrating the same subject and perhaps made about the same time.

1880: THE TRIUMPHANT ENTRY INTO JERUSALEM — a terracotta panel, c. 16″ (40.5 cm) wide x 8″ (20 cm) high, modelled as a sketch for the large panel next described.

This small sketch is now fixed in the inside rear wall of the Baptist Church, Wraysbury, referred to above.

1880: THE TRIUMPHANT ENTRY INTO JERUSALEM — a terracotta panel, c. 120" (305 cm) wide x 40" (101.5 cm) high, exhibited at the Royal Academy in 1881.

Jesus was shown seated on an unbridled ass's colt, preceded by the mother ass which is led by an attendant. Among the many other figures depicted were the Virgin Mary, Lazarus, Judas, Roman soldiers and a child holding a garland. A negro, a Syrian and a Persian illustrate the inscribed text (one of several), "Behold the world is gone after him."

Tinworth introduces a thief, trying to steal a spectator's purse, Judas already receiving the thirty pieces of silver for his betrayal of Jesus, and a disapproving father trying to take away from his son the palm branch he is carrying. A hen and chickens in the foreground is to remind one of Jesus' address to the city of Jerusalem (Matthew xxiii).

This panel is now in the V & A Museum.

1880: DAVID — a terracotta panel, c. 20" (50.8 cm) wide x 50" (127 cm) high, designed and executed for a monument in Wells Cathedral, Somerset, in memory of the South African campaigns of 1878-1879 of the 13th (Prince Albert's) Light Infantry. It forms part of the screen erected by Lord Mark Kerr, K.C.B., colonel of the regiment, and other officers, from a design by B.S. Ferrey, F.S.A.

David is portrayed with a beard and holding a sling. On the left of the panel Tinworth has introduced a frog on a reed. It is interesting to recall that about this time Tinworth began modelling his now famous frog and mice figures as a relaxation from his labours on the large terracotta panels.

1880 SELF-PORTRAIT — a terracotta medallion-portrait of the sculptor, c. 8½" (21.5 cm) diameter. It has a border inscription in Tinworth's familiar lettering: "He hath put down the mighty from their seats and exalted them of low degree."

An example is in the Willett Collection in the Brighton Art Gallery, Sussex.

1881

1881: PREPARING FOR THE CRUCIFIXION — a terracotta panel, c. 144" (366 cm) wide x 62" (157.5 cm) high. A dramatic and powerful composition, embracing no fewer than 50 figures.

Jesus, in the centre, was pictured by Tinworth being disrobed by Roman soldiers, while Simon of Cyrene — who helped bear the cross — kneels reverently before him. A soldier in the foreground, who has been digging the hole to receive the cross, rests against the beam and looks up sympathetically at Jesus. Also in the composition are the Virgin, her sister, and Mary Magdalene accompanied by John, the beloved disciple. The centurion, Nicodemus, Joseph of Arimathea, and Simon Peter (in an attitude of repentance) are also featured. A woman holds out her dead child towards Jesus, hoping for a miracle. The crowd of spectators is held back by Roman soldiers.

This immense work was found too large to be shown at the Royal Academy, but was exhibited at the Conduit Street Gallery in 1883. Tinworth had been told that if the Academy accepted the panel they would have to turn out the work of six other artists to make room for it. Tinworth took the decision very much to heart. "That", he commented, "was a polite way of refusing it. An academician would not study half-a-dozen outsiders if it was his work." Tinworth always considered this panel his greatest work — but hoped to create an even greater one with the long projected GETHSEMANE which, unfortunately, was never finished.

This panel is now in the possession of the South London Art Gallery, Peckham Road, London S.E.5.

1882

c. 1874-c. 1882: During this period, Tinworth modelled a large number of small terracotta panels, some of which were probably intended as sketches for larger projects. The sizes of these panels, as recorded by different sources, vary mostly between 12¼" (31 cm) and 13¼" (33.5 cm) in width and 5¼" (13.3 cm) and 6½" (16.5 cm) in height. Copies of these panels may vary (usually only slightly) in certain details because of Tinworth's practice of working them over in the clay state before firing, sometimes even adding further texts or personal comments.

(References to the passages in the Bible which the panels were intended to illustrate are given in brackets. If one has the curiosity to look them up, they will be found to show very strikingly Tinworth's profound knowledge of the Scriptures.)

(1) THE FINDING OF MOSES (Exodus ii, 8 and 9);
(2) THE TAKING OF SAMSON (I Corinthians x, 12, and Hebrews xi, 8);
(3) DAVID'S LAW (I Samuel xxx, 24);
(4) THE JUDGMENT OF SOLOMON (I Kings iii, 26, and Proverbs xxv, 2);
(5) THE SHUNAMITE'S CHILD (II Kings iv, 18 and 19 and Job ii, 10);
(6) THE MASSACRE OF THE INNOCENTS (Matthew ii, 16 and Ecclesiastes iv, I);
(7) THE FINDING OF JESUS IN THE TEMPLE (Luke ii, 48 and 49, and John v, 39);
(8) OVERTHROWING THE TABLES OF THE MONEY-CHANGERS (John ii, 13 to 15);
(9) THE TRIBUTE MONEY (Matthew xvii, 27);
(10) THE RAISING OF LAZARUS (John xi, 44; John xx, 29; and Psalm lxviii, 20);
(11) THE MARRIAGE FEAST AT CANA (John ii, 1 to 10);
(12) THE LESSON IN HUMILITY (Matthew xviii, 2 and 3, and I Peter v, 6);
(13) THE ANGELS BRINGING LOT AND HIS FAMILY OUT OF SODOM AND GOMORRAH (Genesis xix, 12-17 and Psalms xxxvii). In addition to the biblical references, Tinworth incised "Take heed unto thyself, be sober and watch to the end."
(14) THE FOUR LEPERS OUTSIDE SAMARIA (II Kings, vii, 3, and Psalm cvii);
(16) ZACCHAEUS (Luke xix, 6);
(17) THE LAST SUPPER (Matthew xxvi, 22; John vi, 70; and Judges v, 16);
(18) THE AGONY IN THE GARDEN (Luke xxii, 43; Solomon v, 2; and Mark xiv, 38);
(19) CHRIST BEARING THE CROSS (John xix, 17, and Luke xxiii, 26);
(20) SEALING THE TOMB (Matthew xxvii, 66, and Jonah ii, 6);
(21) THE INCREDULITY OF ST. THOMAS (John xx, 27, and Romans viii, 24);
(22) THE RELEASE OF ST. PETER (I John v, 14);

(23) THE FORTY WHO BOUND THEMSELVES WITH AN OATH (Acts xxiii, 12-35);
(24) THE RESURRECTION (I Corinthians xv, 20; John xx, 1; and II Timothy ii, 6);
(25) PETER'S DENIAL (John xviii, 27; Luke xxii, 61; Hebrews xii, 3; and Romans iii, 27);
(26) DAVID WITH THE HEAD OF GOLIATH (I Samuel xvii, 57; and Psalms lxxv, 7);
(27) THE ADORATION OF THE SHEPHERDS (Luke ii, 16; and Psalms lxviii, 11 and 13);
(28) THE ADORATION OF THE MAGI (Matthew ii, 11 and Isaiah lx, 3).
(29) THE BROW OF THE HILL (Luke iv, 29 and 30);
(30) THE HEM OF THE GARMENT (Mark v, 27, and I Peter i, 7);
(31) THE DAUGHTER OF HERODIAS (Mark vi, 27, and James iii, 8) also described as SALOME DEMANDING THE HEAD OF JOHN THE BAPTIST;
(32) CHRIST BLESSING LITTLE CHILDREN (Matthew xix, 13-15, and Solomon vi, 2 and 3);
(33) THE RELEASE OF BARABBAS (Luke xxiii, 25, and Acts iv, 28);
(34) THE REMORSE OF JUDAS (Matthew xxvii, 3 and 4, and Proverbs xvi, 4);
(35) PAUL AND BARNABUS AT LYSTRA (Acts xiv, 14, and Romans x, 2);
(36) THE ENTRY INTO JERUSALEM (Matthew xxi, 5, and Numbers xxi, 17);
(37) THE BINDING OF SIMEON (Genesis xlii, 24).

The original panels of 25, 28, 29, 30, 31, 32, 33 and 36 were exhibited at the Royal Academy in 1875.

Originals, or copies, of 12, 16, 19, 27, 30 and 31 are illustrated in Dennis No. I, under reference numbers 672, 673, 669, 671, 670 and 674 respectively; also a salt-glaze stoneware version of 24 under No. 661.

Originals or copies of 2, 4, 5, 13 and 14 are in the Minet Library; of 18 in the Brighton Art Gallery, Sussex; and of 21, 25 and 35 in the Sydney Museum. See also Plates 61, 62 and 63 for illustrations of subjects 31, 20 and 6.

Another panel of THE PRODIGAL SON modelled, about the same period, is recorded as being 18" (45.7 cm) wide x 6½" (16.5 cm) high.

In THE MARRIAGE FEAST AT CANA Tinworth portrayed a boy tasting the liquor with his finger to see if it has really become wine. In THE TRIBUTE MONEY children are shown peering into the fish's mouth in the hope no doubt of finding yet another coin. In the ZACCHAEUS panel, Bartimaeus, who has just had his sight restored, is seen reading a scroll. A moving detail in THE MASSACRE OF THE INNOCENTS is the baby whom his mother has hidden in a tree, hoping it may thus avoid being slaughtered. In THE RELEASE OF PETER the apostle is shown knocking at the door of the very house where prayers are being offered for his release; Rhoda says: "It is Peter", but others do not believe this. "Just like us", comments Tinworth. These are but a few examples of the sculptor's imaginative approach to the biblical narratives.

1880-1882: Five terracotta panels, 6" (15.2 cm) square, depicting the following:

(1) THE DISMISSAL OF HAGAR AND ISHMAEL (Genesis xxi, 14);
(2) SAMUEL BROUGHT TO ELI (I Samuel i, 24);
(3) FINDING THE BODY OF THE MAN OF GOD (I Kings xii, 28 and 29, and II Corinthians xi, 26). In a version of this panel in the Minet Library, Knatchbull Road, London, SE5. Tinworth has incised the comment: "The man is taken and the donkey left. It often happens so. Perils among false brethern."
(4) REBEKAH AND ABRAHAM'S SERVANT (Genesis xxiv, 15-20);
(5) JESUS, MARY AND MARTHA (Luke x, 38-42);
(6) THE WHEELWRIGHT'S SHOP: a smaller and slightly different version of the plaque, 8" (20.3 cm) square, already noted under the year 1877.

c. 1880-1882: Small terracotta panels, c. 8" (20.3 cm) square. There are slight variations in size due no doubt to differences of shrinkage in firing:

(1) THE UNJUST JUDGE (Luke xviii, 2-8);
On a panel with this title, in the Minet Library, London SE5, Tinworth has inscribed: "Hold fast till I come. If any man draw back, my soul shall have no pleasure in him." On the door he has put the personal remark: "Mr. Graball no money no hope", which has no direct connection with the parable.
(2) THE DEATH OF ELI (I Samuel iv, 18);
(3) THE SEVEN SONS OF SCEVA (Acts xix, 13-16);
The version in the Minet Library has the strange incised comment: "Is your eye concentrated this time on the central figure?" (This man is the man with an evil spirit);
(4) GETHSEMANE (Luke xxii, 43, and Isiah liii);
(5) THE SAVIOUR AND WOMAN AT THE WELL (John iv, 7-39);
(6) THE SERMON ON THE MOUNT (Matthew v, vi and vii);
(7) CHRIST HEALING THE SICK (Matthew viii and ix);
(8) CALVARY (Matthew xxvii, 35);
(9) THE RESURRECTION OF CHRIST (John xv, 1);
Versions of 1, 2 and 3 are in the Minet Library, and of 5 to 9 in a pulpit in the United Reform Church, East Sheen, Mortlake, London. See also Dennis I, 665 and 666.

1882: THE RELEASE OF BARABBAS (also known as LEAVING THE JUDGMENT HALL), c. 144" (366 cm) wide x 68" (173 cm) high.

Pilate is seen in the centre, pronouncing judgment on Jesus; his wife stands behind him and on each side are attendants holding a bowl of water and a towel. Peter is being held back by a soldier and, on the left, Barabbas is being set free. A palm branch lying on the ground is a bitter reminder of the recent triumphant entry of Jesus into Jerusalem. By the broken vessel and the fallen capital in the foreground Tinworth symbolises the passing of the old dispensation.

The texts quoted are: Acts iv, 27 and 28; Genesis i, 20; Matthew xxvii, 24; Psalms cxli, 6; II Corinthians, ii, 2; Ecclesiastes viii, 12 and 13; and Genesis xlv, 5.

Tinworth described this — one of his most ambitious panels — as "an instantaneous inspiration". It came to him, he said, just as the closing bell was ringing at the Lambeth Pottery at 6 p.m. and he was preparing to leave the building. He went back to his studio and sketched out the entire composition in less than two hours. When he came to the actual large-scale modelling, he did not find it necessary to alter any of the groupings, although a few minor details were added.

1882: AT EVENING TIME IT SHALL BE LIGHT — a terracotta panel, c. 48" (120 cm) wide x 16" (40 cm) high. Now in the Sydney Museum.

1883: THE MEETING OF JACOB AND JOSEPH IN THE LAND OF GOSHEN — a terracotta panel, c. 50" (127 cm) wide x 18" (45.7 cm) high, exhibited in the Royal Academy in 1883.

In this over-elaborated panel, now in the Sydney Museum, there are some 60 figures modelled in high relief, besides numerous cattle, camels, asses and other details.

1883: THE BRAZEN SERPENT — a terracotta panel designed and executed for Sandringham Church, Norfolk, at the request of the then Prince of Wales (later King Edward VII). This church is where the Royal Family have worshipped since Queen Victoria's time when staying at their residence at Sandringham House.

The pole supporting the large image of the serpent occupies the centre of the panel while Moses stands nearby with uplifted rod. A Levite is helping to place the pole in position and another sounds a trumpet.

Tinworth modelled another version of the same incident, with the title THE POWER OF FAITH, for the Bromley-Davenport memorial in 1886.

A small panel entitled MOSES AND THE BRAZEN SERPANT (sic) in the Sydney Museum, may have been a sketch for the Sandringham panel.

1880-1883: Low-relief terracotta panels, c. 8¼" (21 cm) square:

(1) ADAM DISCOVERING EVE;
(2) ADAM AND EVE DRIVEN OUT OF EDEN;
(3) SAMSON THROWING DOWN THE PILLARS;
(4) OUR SAVIOUR IN THE MANGER;
(5) THE HOLY FAMILY IN EGYPT;
(6) AFTER THE BAPTISM.

A variant of 3 is shown in Dennis I, 663.

1884: THE SONS OF CYDIPPE — a terracotta panel in flat relief, c. 67" (170 cm) wide x 31" (79 cm) high. One of the very few panels by Tinworth the subject of which was not inspired by a biblical story.

The idea of the panel came to Tinworth after reading a poem by Edmund (later Sir Edmund) Gosse. On July 12, 1883 he wrote to Gosse: "I am very glad to hear that you are pleased with the sketch that I made from your very clever poem . . . I shall want to write my text on the panel: 'A zeal for God but not according to knowledge.' I should like to make a good panel of it to repay you for the honour that you have done me." (He is referring to the Conduit Street Gallery Exhibition for which Gosse wrote the introduction to the catalogue.)

The story of THE SONS OF CYDIPPE is briefly this: Cydippe, the priestess of Juno at Argo, was once unable to find oxen to draw her chariot to take her to the temple. Her sons, Cleobis and Biton yoked themselves to the chariot and thus took her there amid the applause of the populace, who congratulated Cydippe on having such loving sons.

Cydippe asked Juno to reward her sons with the best gift that could be accorded to mortals, whereupon they fell into a deep sleep from which they never awakened.

It is interesting to notice that although this was not a biblical story, Tinworth told Gosse quite categorically that he would want to write his biblical text on the panel. Cydippe and her sons, so far as Tinworth was concerned, were worshipping the wrong god.

In addition to the panel presented to Gosse, at least one other copy was made. This was presented to Henry (later Sir Henry) Doulton and for many years was in his country home at Woolpits, near Ewhurst, Surrey.

See Plates 58, 59 and 60.

1884: DELIVERANCE AT LAST — a terracotta panel modelled in high relief, 10″ (25.4 cm) wide x 7¾″ (19.7 cm) high. This panel depicting a favourite theme of Tinworth, Moses and Miriam at the Red Sea, exists in at least two versions. One of them is in the Sydney Museum.

1884: HAMAN AND MORDECAI — a terracotta panel based on the story in Esther vi. Other texts quoted are Luke ix, 55; John iv, 10; and Psalms ii, 6.

Haman is shown leading the King's horse, with Mordecai seated on it, through the city street. Onlookers, attracted by Haman's proclamation, appear from all directions — expressing by their attitudes reactions of wonder, envy or gladness.

1884: THE QUEEN OF EDWARD THE FOURTH PARTING WITH HER SON.

EDWARD THE FOURTH MEETING LADY GRAY.

Two unusual Tinworth panels in flat-relief terracotta portraying scenes from popular Victorian history books, such as Agnes Strickland's "Lives of the Queens of England". How Tinworth came to model these panels remains so far a mystery. No further details have been discovered although photographs exist of both panels (See Figure 25).

c. 1884: JACOB REPROVING SIMEON AND LEVI — a terracotta panel, c. 10″ (25.4 cm) wide x 6¼″ (15.9 cm) high.

The incident represented in this panel is narrated in Genesis xxxiv.

1884: THE LAST SUPPER — a terracotta panel, 48″ (122 cm) wide x 16″ (40.5 cm) high, designed and executed for the reredos of the Priory Church, Bury St. Edmunds, at Walsham-le-Willows, Suffolk — where it still remains in good condition.

An interesting feature of this panel is that Tinworth has departed from the usual treatment of the subject by showing Jesus standing instead of sitting after saying "One of you will betray me." Most of the disciples have sprung to their feet after exclaiming "Lord, is it I?" but Judas remains seated, his head turned away from Jesus. The sculptor has inscribed the words "All capable of faithlessness and treason."

1884: TOUCH ME NOT — a semi-circular terracotta panel, c. 72" (183 cm) diameter x 42" (106.6 cm) high, designed and executed for Tisbury Parish Church, near Salisbury, Wiltshire — where it still remains in good condition.

It depicts Mary Magdalene talking to Jesus, whom she at first assumes to be the gardener.

An alternative title is A RESURRECTION MEETING.

Fig. 25. Terra-cotta panel: *"Edward the Fourth Meeting Lady Gray".*

1885: THE DAUGHTER OF HERODIAS DEMANDING THE HEAD OF JOHN THE BAPTIST — a large terracotta panel representing the same subject that Tinworth had first approached in a small panel shown at the Royal Academy in 1875.

King Herod is depicted overcome with grief at the consequence of his rash promise, while Herodias, his wife, encourages Salome to persist in her request. A monkey is shown peeping out at the scene from a Greek vase, which has inscribed on it by Tinworth: "The monkey in our nature."

1885: THE HOLY WOMEN AT THE SEPULCHRE — a terracotta panel, c. 96" (244 cm) wide x 30" (76 cm) high, executed for a reredos under the east window of the Marquess of Northampton's private chapel at Castle Ashby.

One of the few panels for which a sketch was provided by the client. Tinworth, however, altered it and added extra figures. The panel was removed when alterations were made to the chapel in 1936; its present whereabouts is not known.

1885: THE ANOINTING AT BETHANY — a terracotta panel, c. 55″ (139.7 cm) wide x 24″ (61 cm) high.

In this panel Tinworth has regarded the accounts given by Matthew and Mark of the anointing in the house of Simon the Leper as relating to a similar event at the home of Lazarus as recorded in John's gospel.

Lazarus is seated next to Jesus and Judas is rising to his feet to complain of what he regards as waste of the precious ointment. Simon is shown seated with his back to the spectator, his head having been shaved in accordance with the law of Moses for purification from leprosy. Martha is looking after the guests seated at a table.

Discrepancies in the story of the anointing have been seized upon by critics of Christianity — but Tinworth was not worried by them. What mattered to him was how Jesus responded to the situation, wherever it may have taken place.

This panel was designed and erected as a memorial to the Duke of Sutherland in the Parish Church of St. Mary and All Saints, Trentham, Staffordshire — where it still remains.

1885: THE TAKING OF SAMSON BY THE PHILISTINES — a terracotta panel, c. 52″ (132 cm) wide x 22″ (56 cm) high.

This shows the Philistines binding Samson while Delilah stands mocking. The barber is seen leaving on the left with Samson's shorn locks. The surprise, horror and despair of the enfeebled Samson are vividly portrayed.

Tinworth has treated this subject at least twice before in small panels, examples of which are in the Brighton Art Gallery and the Sydney Museum.

1885: SIR EDWIN CHADWICK — a portrait bust in terracotta of the man known as "the father of English Sanitation" because of the leading role he played in the Sanitary Reform Movement of the 1840s and 1850s.

The bust was exhibited at the Royal Academy in 1885 and was described by a critic in the "Daily Telegraph" as "one of those strongly independent productions which, without disparagement to their artistic quality, may be described as anti-classic."

See Chapter III for Tinworth's comments on Chadwick.

1885: ABRAHAM AT THE DOOR OF HIS TENT RECEIVING VISITORS — a terracotta panel, 36″ (91.5 cm) square, designed and executed for fixing above the entrance porch to Sir Henry Doulton's country residence, "Woolpits", near Ewhurst, Surrey.

When the porch was demolished in 1935, the panel was presented to the Sydney Museum.

1885: CHRIST THE HEALER — a panel with this title was reported as being in process during 1885, but further details are not at present known.

1885: SAUL ATTEMPTING THE LIFE OF DAVID — a terracotta panel, probably a fairly large one, representing the scene recorded in I Samuel xix.

The King is depicted just after throwing the javeline at David, who had been playing the harp before him. Jonathan, Saul's son, rises to remonstrate with his father, while Michal, David's wife, turns towards her husband in alarm.

1885: NEBUCHADNEZZAR ORDERING SHADRACH, MESHACH AND ABED-NEGO INTO THE FURNACE — a terracotta panel, c. 26" (66 cm) wide x 13" (33 cm) high, representing the miracle recorded in Daniel iii, 15.

This panel, also described as THE THREE CHILDREN IN THE FIERY FURNACE, is now in the Parish Church of St. Mary, Alsager, Cheshire.

Tinworth added a personal inscription: "May God save old England from image worship either of gold or any other material." (The three men — why they should be described as children is not clear, unless "children of the Lord" was in Tinworth's mind — had been condemned to the furnace by King Nebuchadnezzar because they refused to worship the golden image.)

1885: THE MIRACULOUS DRAUGHT OF FISHES — a terracotta panel, c. 58" (147 cm) wide x 29" (73.7 cm) high, designed and executed to form part of the reredos of Holy Trinity Church, Bengeo, Hertford — where it still remains.

The panel, also known as CHILDREN, HAVE YE ANY MEAT?, shows the apostles drawing the net to shore while Christ stands in the centre of the boat, bearing the marks of nails on his hands and feet. John, the beloved disciple, kneels in adoration before him. On the shore is a small fire with fishes laid upon it. The scene is based upon John xxi, 1-14.

1886

1886: GENESIS — a terracotta frieze, c. 50" (127 cm) wide x 14½" (37 cm) high, exhibited in 1886 at the Grosvenor Gallery, London.

The frieze — an unusual design for Tinworth — portrays some of the principal events described in the first book of the Bible, interwoven within the letters of the word GENESIS. These scenes include;"The Fall;" "The Murder of Abel;" "Eve with children at her knee", "The Deluge", "The Offering of Isaac", "Jacob's Ladder" and "The Selling of Joseph".

Several copies of this frieze were made; Tinworth was working on one of them as late as 1895. An example is in the City Museum and Art Gallery, Hanley, Stoke-on-Trent, Staffordshire.

1886: EXODUS — a terracotta frieze similar in size and conception to the one just described.

The incidents represented include: "The Finding of Moses"; "Moses and Aaron before Pharaoh"; "The Death of the First-Born"; "Moses' flight into the land of Midian"; "The Egyptians pursuing the Israelites through the Red Sea"; "The Song of Miriam" and "The Worship of the Golden Calf."

An example of this frieze is also in the City Museum and Art Gallery, Hanley.

1886: THE PRODIGAL SON — a terracotta panel, c. 120" (304.8 cm) wide x 40" (101.6 cm) high, based on a small sketch made several years earlier.

Tinworth was not satisfied with the first panel when it came from the kiln and did another before he would allow it to be shown at an exhibition in Doulton's Lambeth showroom in August 1887.

There were over 30 figures in this panel, displaying a remarkable variety of individual stances and expressions. Characteristic of Tinworth's imaginative approach to all his scriptural panels are the child examining the prodigal's old worn shoes, the people peering through the lattice and the unbelieving expression on the face of the elder brother.

1886: Four low-relief terracotta panels, c. 34" (86.4 cm) wide x 86" (218.5 cm) high, designed and executed for a memorial to Mr. William Bromley-Davenport, M.P., in the private family Chapel at Capesthorne, near Macclesfield, Cheshire — where they still are in good condition. The chapel is said to be the earliest surviving architectural work of John Wood of Bath, who designed it when he was only 18.

The panels were entitled by Tinworth: THE POWER OF DARKNESS (a representation of the Crucifixion); THE POWER OF LIGHT (the Ascension); THE POWER OF TEMPTATION (the Garden of Eden) and THE POWER OF FAITH (the brazen serpent raised in the wilderness).

Among the interesting features of these panels may be mentioned: Adam asleep with one arm resting on the back of an elephant, upon which Eve is climbing in order to reach the forbidden fruit. Tinworth explained that he showed Adam asleep but Eve wide-awake and fully conscious of what she was doing. He quoted as his authority for this I Timothy, ii, 14: "And Adam was not deceived, but the woman being deceived was in the transgression."

In THE POWER OF FAITH panel Tinworth represented Moses standing by the side of the pole on which is an image of the venomous serpent that had caused suffering and death among the Hebrews. Fiery serpents are shown flying in all directions. In the foreground lies an Israelite who has been bitten but is recovering after having looked at the brazen serpent. Apparently unaware of any danger, his little child is climbing up on him. Tinworth regarded the children as being immune from danger from the plague of serpents, not having shared in the sin which preceded it.

When the panels were completed, the press and many distinguished visitors were invited to Tinworth's studio to see them. A critic remarked that he had forgotten to put any scales on the brazen serpent, whereupon Tinworth retorted: "Do you think *they* had time?"

1887: THE LAST SUPPER — a terracotta panel, c. 73" (185 cm) wide x 33" (84 cm) high, designed and executed for the reredos of St. Peter's Church, Jersey, Channel Islands. Like the smaller panel at Walsham-le-Willows executed in 1884, this one is basically on the text "Lord, is it I?" (Matthew xxvi, 22).

1887: LOVEST THOU ME? — a terracotta panel, c. 81" (206 cm) wide x 38" (96.5 cm) high, designed and executed to fit within one of the arches in the same church as THE LAST SUPPER described above.

This panel, in which Peter, the patron saint of the church, features prominently, is based on the post-Resurrection scene at the Sea of Galilee described in John xxi, 15-17.

1887: Terracotta study of the head and shoulders of an elderly bearded man, thought perhaps to be Moses.

1887: CHRIST BEFORE HEROD — a terracotta panel, c. 276″ (701 cm) wide x 108″ (274 cm) high.

   This, the most ambitious and largest of all Tinworth's completed panels, was the final expression of a theme which he had had in mind for many years and for which he had sketched in a number of small panels — none of which satisfied him.

Fig. 26. Portrait of George Tinworth working on the terra-cotta panel: *"Christ before Herod,"* 1887.

The panel, all the figures in which are life-size, depicts Herod seeking to question the silent Jesus, as related in Luke xxiii, 9. Herod hopes to see some miracle performed and Tinworth has assumed that some sick people were brought into the palace with that end in mind.

In a letter to the editor of the magazine "Sunday at Home", dated 17th September, 1889, Tinworth wrote: "Before I commenced the panel CHRIST BEFORE HEROD I was coming home from the seaside, having had to go away for my health. The train had got about half-way home when a young infidel got in and commenced a conversation with a young woman, and I could not say a word to stop him, which upset me very much. So I know a little of what Christ must have suffered all that time he was silent before Herod. So, to Herod he could not and would not open his mouth but to doubting Thomas he would open his side."

Some of Tinworth's fellow-artists at Lambeth, while respecting his views and never doubting his sincerity, found him to be what one of them called "an uncomfortable companion" because of his puritanical outlook and behaviour. He would, for instance, attend the annual cricket match at Sir Henry Doulton's country residence, as he thought it would be rude to refuse the invitation. But, instead of watching the game with any great interest, he would sit under a tree and read his Bible.

1888

1888: Terracotta reredos for St. Mary's Parish Church, Lambeth, London, S.E.I. Presented by Sir Henry Doulton as a memorial to his wife and to his father, John Doulton, founder of the Doulton enterprise.

The reredos originally comprised three arched panels in terracotta separated and bordered by salt-glaze stoneware columns. The church was bombed during World War II and the two side panels containing terracotta figures of Moses, Elijah, Peter and Paul were ruined beyond repair. Only the central panel, depicting THE CRUCIFIXION now remains.

Also in this church are two smaller panels, dated 1888 and 1899, which will be described later.

1888: A similar reredos to the one just described and now in St. Philip's Church, Barbados, West Indies. This was originally made for St. Mary's, Lambeth. But it proved too large for the space available and Tinworth had to do another.

1888: Terracotta panel, c. 36" (91.5 cm) wide x 51" (129.5 cm) high, incorporating a portrait of LORD SHAFTESBURY, the famous Victorian philanthropist and social reformer.

This panel was originally designed and executed for the Shaftesbury Institute in Shaftesbury Avenue, London, W.C. It was removed in 1959 to the Shaftesbury Society's Victoria School for Crippled Children in Bournemouth, Dorsetshire (See Figure 13).

1888: SIR HENRY DOULTON — a portrait bust in terracotta, 18" (45.5 cm) high, now in the Doulton Collection at Stoke-on-Trent.

1888: REBEKAH RECEIVING GIFTS FROM ABRAHAM'S SERVANT — a terracotta panel, 20½" (51.75 cm) wide x 13" (32.75 cm) high.

See Plate 56 for details. Tinworth had earlier used the same subject in a small panel made between 1880 and 1882.

1888: SIR PHILIP CUNLIFFE-OWEN — a portrait bust in terracotta of Sir Philip, who was director of the South Kensington Museum (later the Victoria & Albert Museum).

Sir Philip was a great admirer of Tinworth, who found him, however, a troublesome sitter — as he did not always keep his appointments in time. The bust was shown at the Paris Exhibition of 1889, where some journalists mistook it for a bust of the Prince of Wales.

1888: THOMAS A. EDISON — a portrait bust in terracotta of the famous American inventor, described in Mrs. Tinworth's diary as "the inventor of a voice machine".

1888: Reredos, pulpit and font in terracotta and salt-glaze stoneware for the English church of St. Alban, Copenhagen, Denmark.

The centre panel of the reredos, 41″ (104 cm) high, depicts THE ASCENSION and the side panels, both 35″ (89 cm) high, CHRIST APPEARING TO ST. THOMAS and THE BETRAYAL. The four panels on the font, 10″ (25.4 cm) high, show CHRIST BLESSING LITTLE CHILDREN; THE FINDING OF MOSES; HANNAH BRINGING SAMUEL TO ELI; and THE SAVIOUR IN THE MANGER.

The overall design was by A.W. Blomfield, M.A., but Tinworth chose the subjects for the panels and interpreted them independently.

1888: SAMUEL MORLEY — a semi-circular portrait panel, in low relief terracotta, of the well-known social reformer and educationalist — designed to go over the entrance to Morley College in Westminster Bridge Road, London, S.E.1|(See Figure 14).

Morley was shown surrounded by students, to one of whom he is handing a prize. The panel was destroyed when the college was hit by a bomb in 1943.

1888: PHARAOH SENDING ABRAHAM AND SARAH AWAY — a small terracotta panel representing the scene narrated in Genesis xii, 10-20.

1888: CHRIST BLESSING LITTLE CHILDREN — a small terracotta panel, c. 24″ (61 cm) wide x 13″ (33 cm) high.

This panel, based on Matthew xix, 13-15, is in the former Parish Church of St. Mary, next to the gateway of Lambeth Palace.

1888: THE ASCENSION — a terracotta panel, 25″ (63.5 cm) wide x 42″ (106.7 cm) high, designed and executed for the Church of St. Mary Magdalene, Trinity Road, Wandsworth, London — where it may still be seen.

One of four or more different interpretations by Tinworth of the scene described in Luke xxiv, 50-51 and Mark xvi, 19.

1888: THE GOOD SAMARITAN — a terracotta panel designed and executed for the chapel of St. Thomas' Hospital, Lambeth, London, S.E.1., as a memorial to Mrs. Wardroper, Matron of the hospital 1854-1887.

1889

1889: MADONNA AND HOLY CHILD — a terracotta figure in a terracotta niche, modelled from a design by A.W. Blomfield, A.R.A., and shown at the Paris Exhibition of 1889.

This was one of the rare occasions when Tinworth worked from somebody else's design.

1889: a large terracotta JARDINIERE decorated in a relief with a band of children in triumphal procession.

1890

1890: BOY WITH PITCHER — a terracotta figure of a boy holding a pitcher, with a swan at his feet; also terracotta figures of a WOMAN WITH CHILDREN and a GIRL. These three figures were apparently intended to form part of a fountain.

(In addition to special pieces which bear his monogram, Tinworth is known to have designed for general reproduction a number of other jardinieres, vases, fountains, figures, window-boxes, sundials, and other garden ornaments. See also the fountain described later under the dates 1897-1899.)

1892: THE OVERTHROW OF PHAROAH AND HIS HOST IN THE RED SEA — a terracotta panel, c. 67″ (170.2 cm) wide x 25″ (63.5 cm) high. Described in a Doulton publication dated April, 1892, as "one of the most vigorous of Mr. Tinworth's recent productions."

The panel is dominated by the towering wall of water at the back of the panel, about to engulf the Egyptian army. Fish are seen within the wall of water and birds hover overhead. The Pharaoh is represented in the centre, standing in his chariot. The general confusion is illustrated by horses and men prostrate on the ground, chariots overturned and wheels loosened.

The texts quoted are Exodus, xiv, 22, 23, and 27, and Matthew vii, 2. Now in the chapel of the North Staffordshire Royal Infirmary, Stoke-on-Trent.

1891

1891-1892 PROFESSOR HENRY FAWCETT, M.P. — a terracotta memorial to Fawcett, popularly known as "the blind Postmaster-General."

This impressive memorial, nearly 200″ (508 cm) high, including the 90″ (228.5 cm) plinth, was erected in Vauxhall Park, Lambeth, London, S.E.1., on the site of Fawcett's old house. It was unveiled by the then Archbishop of Canterbury on 7th June, 1893.

Fawcett was depicted seated, in academic robes; behind him was a winged figure of "Victory" extending a wreath of laurels. Round the base, eight bas-reliefs symbolising: "Courage", Sympathy", "Justice", "Truth", and other subjects (See Figure 15).

The memorial was unfortunately vandalised and eventually removed from the park. What then became of it is not known.

1892

1892: HISTORY OF ENGLAND VASE — designed for exhibition at the Chicago, U.S.A. World Fair of 1893.

See Plates 52 through 55.

1893

1893: ELIJAH BEING FED BY THE RAVEN — a terracotta panel based on the story told in I Kings xvii, 6.

An interesting feature of this panel is that Tinworth had depicted the raven bringing the food from the table of King Ahab, who was Elijah's persecutor.

1893: THE TAMING OF THE SHREW — a terracotta panel illustrating a scene from Shakespeare's play of this name. It was in the foyer of the Old Vic Theatre, Waterloo Road, London, for many years, but it disappeared during reconstruction operations.

It is believed that Tinworth did some other panels based on plays of Shakespeare, but no definite information has so far been traced.

Fig. 27. Terra-cotta panel: *"The Taming of the Shrew".*

1893: THE LIFE OF JOSEPH — a series of 25 small terracotta panels, representing scenes from the Genesis story of Joseph. These were begun some time earlier and completed in 1893. They were originally intended to be shown at the Chicago World Fair of 1893, but apparently were not ready in time. The subjects are:

(1) JACOB INTRODUCING RACHEL AND THE CHILD JOSEPH TO ESAU;
(2) JOSEPH TELLING JACOB ABOUT THE SONS OF BILHAH AND ZILPAH;
(3) JOSEPH TELLING HIS DREAM TO HIS BROTHERS;
(4) JOSEPH LEAVING HIS FATHER'S HOUSE;
(5) JOSEPH ENQUIRING WHITHER HIS BRETHREN HAD GONE;
(6) JOSEPH FINDING HIS BRETHREN IN DOTHAN;
(7) JOSEPH IN THE PIT;
(8) JOSEPH SOLD TO THE MIDIANITES;

- (9) JOSEPH'S COAT BROUGHT TO JACOB;
- (10) SELLING JOSEPH TO POTIPHAR;
- (11) JOSEPH'S ESCAPE FROM TEMPTATION;
- (12) JOSEPH IN PRISON INTERPRETING THE DREAMS OF THE BUTLER AND BAKER;
- (13) PHARAOH PUTTING THE RING ON THE HAND OF JOSEPH;
- (14) JOSEPH GATHERING THE CORN IN THE SEVEN YEARS OF PLENTY;
- (15) THE FAMINE;
- (16) JOSEPH'S BRETHREN COMING TO BUY CORN;
- (17) SIMEON IS BOUND AS HOSTAGE FOR BENJAMIN;
- (18) BENJAMIN LEAVING HOME TO GO TO EGYPT;
- (19) JOSEPH ENTERTAINING HIS BRETHREN;
- (20) FINDING THE CUP IN BENJAMIN'S SACK;
- (21) JUDAH PLEADING FOR BENJAMIN;
- (22) JOSEPH MAKING HIMSELF KNOWN TO HIS BRETHREN;
- (23) MEETING OF JACOB AND JOSEPH;
- (24) THE DEATH-BED OF JACOB;
- (25) JOSEPH AND HIS PEOPLE GOING TO BURY THEIR FATHER JACOB.

Copies of these panels were offered for general sale, but there is no record of how many were made — probably not a large number. Tinworth described them as "not greatly elaborated".

Copies of 2, 7 and 24 are in the Minet Library.

1894: CHRIST IN THE GARDEN OF GETHSEMANE — a sketch model in terracotta for a large panel which Tinworth had had in mind for many years. This panel is said to have been intended to be of "giant proportions" with life-size figures.

1894: MATTHEW — a terracotta frieze designed along similar lines to the GENESIS and EXODUS friezes made in 1886.

1894: CANON LIDDON — a portrait bust in terracotta.

Liddon, a Canon of St. Paul's Cathedral, London, was a famous Victorian preacher and social reformer.

1894: J. PASSMORE EDWARDS — a medallion portrait in terracotta.

Edwards, a former Member of Parliament and well-known as Editor of the "Echo" and other journals, was founder of over seventy schools, hospitals, public libraries and other institutions.

1894: WILLIAM BLADES — a medallion portrait in terracotta.

Blades was a well-known Victorian printer, author and collector of pictures, books and prints. He was an authority on William Caxton and his press.

1894: CHARLES BRADLAUGH — a life-size terracotta statue which still stands in Abington Square, Northhampton — but which has several times been painted over.

Bradlaugh was famous, indeed notorious, for his radical and atheistic views. Elected twice as Member of Parliament, he was not allowed to take his seat because he refused to swear the oath of allegiance on the Bible.

1894: THE REVEREND CHARLES HADDON SPURGEON — a memorial group to the famous non-conformist preacher, commissioned for the Spurgeon Orphanage, Stockwell, London.

The group embraced a life-size terracotta statue of Spurgeon and two terracotta panels, one showing the preacher lecturing to students and the other him talking to children (See Figure 16).

When the orphanage, which suffered bomb damage during World War II, was moved to Birchington in Kent, an unsuccessful attempt was made to dismantle and re-erect the statue. The panels, however, were saved and one is now at Spurgeon's College, South Norwood Hill, London, and the other is in the Spurgeon Orphanage in Birchington.

1894: CHRIST BLESSING THE LITTLE CHILDREN — a large terracotta figure group on a salt-glaze stoneware base, designed and executed for erection in the Whitworth Park, Manchester, England.

Tinworth had a number of children into his studio to pose for this group. Progress was often delayed because he could not resist playing with them. "Very soon", he once said, "they regard me as a kind grandfather."

The group was destroyed, except for the plinth, by a bomb during World War II — one of several of Tinworth's works which met a similar fate.

1895

1895: GEORGE TINWORTH — an oval terracotta portrait plaque, 5¼" (13 cm) wide x 6¼" (15.75 cm) high, depicting the sculptor himself, with his signature and monogram inscribed.

A copy is in the Sydney Museum.

1895: SIR CHARLES CAMERON — a terracotta medallion portrait of the baronet and Member of Parliament, who was also a well-known Scottish physician and social and medical reformer.

1896

1896: THE CRUCIFIXION — a large terracotta panel, c. 60" (15.25 cm) wide x 120" (304.8 cm) high, designed and executed for the Parish Church, Shelton, Stoke-on-Trent.

In 1902, two side panels were added; all three are still there.

1892-1896: Nine terracotta panels, each c. 48" (122 cm) wide x 24" (61 cm) high, featuring scenes from the life of MOSES, as told in Genesis — they are:

(1) THE MOTHER OF MOSES MAKING THE ARK OF BULRUSHES;
(2) THE FINDING OF MOSES AMONG THE RUSHES;
(3) MOSES BROUGHT TO PHARAOH'S DAUGHTER;
(4) MOSES BECOMES THE ADOPTED SON OF PHAROAH'S DAUGHTER;
(5) MOSES ACCUSED BY THE HEBREW;
(6) THE JEWS BRICKMAKING IN EGYPT;
(7) THE JEWS LEAVING EGYPT;
(8) THE OVERTHROW OF PHARAOH AND HIS HOST IN THE RED SEA;
(9) THE SONG OF MIRIAM AT THE RED SEA.

A version of 2 is in the Parish Church of St. John Baptist in Erith, Kent, and one of 6 in the Cuming Museum.

During the period when Tinworth was working on these panels he also modelled for Mr. J. Compton-Ricket, M.P. a group of figures "in the round", depicting the story of THE FINDING OF MOSES and including — as well as the human figures — an ibis, a peacock and some monkeys.

1897

c. 1895-1897: THE BUILDING OF NOAH'S ARK — a large terracotta panel based on the story in Genesis vi-viii. Tinworth told a visitor to his studio that he had had the idea for this panel in his mind for many years.

The ark was placed high up, but, said Tinworth, "however high the waters will reach it." In the front of the ark — and at the base of the panel — Noah harangues a large crowd of people who have come to ask him what he is about. Lower down, revellers are drinking, gambling and cock-fighting.

Tinworth got the idea for the building of the ark, as shown, from a barge-builders' yard on the Thames at Chiswick.

"I want to suggest", he also said, "that Noah's dock-yard would have been a sort of 'bank-holiday' resort for the multitude who, when bent on mischief would, out of spite for Noah, go and practise it under the very shadow of the ark." (See Figure 18).

1897: A small terracotta panel portraying Tinworth standing on the shoulders of a companion and peering into Mr. John Sparkes' studio at the Lambeth School of Art.

This was intended to be one of a series illustrating scenes from the sculptor's early life.

1899

1899: A JESTER — a terracotta figure. See Plate 150.

1899: CONFIDENCE IN FRIENDSHIP — a terracotta panel based on a Greek story.

Alexander the Great is seen drinking a medicinal draught, prepared for him by his friend and personal physician, just after he had received a letter informing him that the doctor had been bribed by the Persians to poison him.

This is one of the few pagan subjects which Tinworth chose for one of his panels. Characteristically, however, he inscribed a biblical text: Hebrews x, 35 — "Cast not away therefore your confidence which hath great recompence of reward."

1899: CHRIST IN THE TEMPLE AS A BOY — a terracotta panel in St. Mary's Church, Lambeth, London, S.E.I.

1899: MICHAL — a terracotta panel, c. 15½" (39.5 cm) wide x 8½" (21.6cm), representing the incident in the life of David which is described in I Samuel xix, 11-17.

Tinworth has inscribed the text:"And Michal took an image and laid it in the bed" together with a comment of his own "Michal, the woman that would not sell you."

1897-1899: Fountain in deep blue and white salt-glaze stoneware, c. 150" (381 cm) high, with circular basin 144" (365.75 cm) in diameter. Six winged figures symbolising: TRUTH, ART; HOPE; COURAGE; INDUSTRY and MUSIC were depicted.

The figures held urns from which flowed water, and the fountain was surmounted by a female figure and a group of children holding water urns. There were also figures of kingfishers, herons and storks in tiers.

The fountain was exhibited at the Doulton showrooms in Lambeth before being sent to the Paris Exhibition of 1900.

1897-1899: Large candelabrum, or "electrolier", in salt-glaze stoneware — mainly brown and white — with tiers of figures having some reference to "Night".

At the base, Tinworth modelled sleeping figures of the FOOLISH VIRGINS; above them a group of Gideon's warriors blowing their trumpets and bearing on their heads pitchers in which they have concealed their lamps (see Judges vii, 16-22). Above these again, a band of small children representing an Eastern marriage procession, and at the top the wakeful WISE VIRGINS of the well-known parable. (Matthew xxv, 1-13).

This candelabrum, also displayed in the Doulton showrooms, and like the fountain, also intended for the Paris Exhibition, was unfortunately damaged in transit, so that only the figures of the WISE AND FOOLISH VIRGINS were shown.

1897-1899: Three terracotta panels in low relief, designed and executed for the reredos of the chapel at St. Thomas' Hospital, Lambeth, London.

The central panel represents: THE ASCENSION OF OUR LORD; the right hand one MARY MAGDALENE AT THE TOMB and the left hand one DOUBTING THOMAS.

These panels were presented by the children of Sir Henry Doulton, in memory of their father, who was a governor and almoner of the hospital from 1876 to 1897. They were unveiled in 1899 by the then Bishop of London, who said in the course of his address that Tinworth's name and that of Sir Henry would always go together.

1899: THE ANGEL APPEARING TO THE SHEPHERDS — a terracotta panel, c. 8¼" (21 cm) square, with inscribed text: "And there were in the same country shepherds abiding in the field, keeping watch over their flock by night." (Luke ii, 8).

1902

1902: THE WISE MEN and THE VISIT OF THE SHEPHERDS — two terracotta panels, 36" (91.5 cm) wide x 84" (213.4 cm) high, designed and executed for Shelton Parish Church. These were to go on either side of the panel of THE CRUCIFIXION erected there in 1896.

1902: THE ENTRY OF THE APOSTLE PAUL INTO ROME — a terracotta panel, c. 112" (284.5 cm) wide x 36" (91.5 cm) high.

Concerning this panel, Tinworth told the "Pottery Gazette" in June 1902: "I was in Rome three or so years ago and I walked three miles up the Appian

Way, and I thought to myself 'Well, I should like to model a panel of Paul coming into Rome.' The head was influenced by a bust of Paul that I saw in the catacombs. He had a bullet-shaped head of his own . . . he looked in that bust like a man who could say: 'You may hit me all day but you won't hurt me.' It was a strong head I can tell you. Paul was no chicken."

Tinworth also called this panel THE TWO MESSENGERS. On the left, he showed a statue of Mercury, representing the old pagan order, while St. Paul, in a chariot drawn by oxen, stood for the new Christian dispensation.

1902: FREEDOM FROM SIN and FREEDOM FROM SLAVERY — two terracotta panels, each c. 39" (99 cm) wide x 55" (139.7 cm) high, designed and executed for the Baptist Church House, Southampton Row, London; erected there when it was built in 1903.

They are still there today, one in the visitor's room and the other in a committee room.

1903

1902-1903: CHRIST'S KINGDOM OF PEACE — a large terracotta panel based on Tinworth's interpretation of Isaiah, xi, 5-9.

Christ is shown in the centre as the Good Shepherd, carrying a lamb. A wolf with a lamb, a leopard and a kid, a calf and a young lion, and a fatling led by little children feature prominently in the design. In the background are angels with outspread wings and trees in between.

This panel was intended for the St. Louis, U.S.A. Exhibition of 1904, but, because of its great size and weight — and the risk of breakage — it was not sent. No record of the actual measurements has been found.

1905

1905: REBEKAH LEAVING HER FATHER'S HOUSE — a terracotta panel which Tinworth told a visitor to his studio in 1905 he had "just finished for an American gentleman who bought some of my panels thirty years before."

In 1881-1882 and in 1888 Tinworth had modelled other panels featuring Rebekah.

1906

1902-1906: Four terracotta panels shown at the New Dudley Gallery, London in 1906 — but perhaps made somewhat earlier:

(1) THE MASTER IS COME AND CALLETH FOR THEE;

(2) CHRIST BLESSING LITTLE CHILDREN;

(3) WEEPING MAY ENDURE FOR A NIGHT BUT JOY COMETH IN THE MORNING;

(4) THOU SHALT NO MORE BE TERMED FORSAKEN.

1907

c. 1900-1907: FROM SUNSET TO SUNSET — a series of 14 terracotta panels, illustrations of which were reproduced in a little book with the sub-title "Our Saviour's last day of Suffering". Many relevant passages from both Old and New Testaments, chosen by Tinworth, accompany each illustration.

Mr. Walter Fairhall, who joined the Lambeth Studios in 1902, recalled that by then Tinworth had already begun work on these panels, which he completed in 1907. The panels were reproduced from moulds by Tinworth's assistants and finished by him. Occasional copies were still being produced up to the time of Tinworth's death in 1913.

The fourteen subjects of the panels are:

(1) THE AGONY IN GETHSEMANE;

(2) THE ARREST IN GETHSEMANE;

(3) CHRIST BEFORE CAIPHAS;

(4) PETER'S DENIAL;

(5) CHRIST GOING BEFORE PILATE;

(6) CHRIST BEFORE HEROD;

(7) CHRIST BEING SCOURGED;

(8) THE EARLY MORNING OF THE LAST DAY;

(9) CHRIST GOING TO BE CRUCIFIED;

(10) SIMON OF CYRENE HELPING CHRIST TO BEAR THE CROSS;

(11) THE THIRD HOUR (The Crucifixion);

(12) THE NINTH HOUR (JESUS DIES);

(13) ALL MISERY PAST (JESUS TAKEN DOWN FROM THE CROSS); (See Figure 19).

(14) THE BURIAL OF CHRIST.

1904

c. 1904-1906: THE GREEK MOTHER — a large terracotta panel depicting the mother giving a shield to her son as he sets out for war, with the words: "Either bring this shield back or be brought back upon it."

This panel was exhibited at the New Dudley Gallery, London, in June 1906. It was later presented by Mr. Henry Lewis Doulton (Sir Henry's only son) to the National Art Gallery in Canberra, Australia. It is now in Parliament House, Canberra (See Figure 20).

c. 1904-1906: PHILIP AND THE ETHIOPIAN EUNUCH — a terracotta panel exhibited at the New Dudley Gallery, London, in June, 1906.

c. 1904-1906: Sketch model for a proposed Shakespeare memorial to be erected in Southwark.

This model, c. 28" (71 cm) wide x 45" (114.3 cm) high, is now in the Cuming Museum. The project for the memorial never came to anything, much to Tinworth's disappointment (See Figures 21 and 28).

1905

c. 1905-1907: DAVID'S PRAYER — a terracotta panel based on Psalm li and on the story of Bathsheba related in II Samuel xi and xiii.

David is lying prostrate on the ground, refusing to be comforted. A little page is vainly offering something to eat. In the corner are seen groups of councillors.

Tinworth read Psalm li and Romans v to his father when he was dying. The psalm begins: "Have mercy upon me, O God, according unto the multitude of thy tender mercies blot out my transgressions." His father said that "if a minister came to him he would push him down the stairs" but he let Tinworth read to him and then said "George, I often say 'God be merciful to me a sinner'." This made Tinworth very happy. Contrary to what some have written, Tinworth had a great affection for his father, who, he said, "was a fine man when he was not under the influence of drink."

At the time of the father's death, the family was almost destitute and they had to bury him in a pauper's grave. Many years later, Tinworth tried in vain to find the grave, as he wanted to erect a memorial stone over it.

Fig. 28. Clay sketches for panels on the Shakespeare Moument (Contemporary photographs in the *Southwark Local Studies Library*).

1907

c. 1907-1910: THE DAUGHTERS OF MANASSEH COMING TO MOSES FOR THEIR PORTION — a terracotta panel based on the incident narrated in Numbers xxvii.

c. 1907-1910: THE SAVIOUR APPEARING TO THE DISCIPLES AFTER THE RESURRECTION — a terracotta panel, c. 120″ (304.8 cm) wide x 72″ (183 cm) high.

The subject of this panel was the incident recorded in John xxi.

c. 1907-1910: CHRIST AT EMMAUS — a terracotta panel, c. 72″ (183 cm) wide x 36″ (92 cm) high.

This panel was ordered by an American lady for erection in the Church of the Mediator in Bronx, New York. U.S.A. Tinworth also referred to it as THE SAVIOUR BREAKING BREAD AT EMMAUS. This appearance of Christ after his resurrection is recorded in Luke xxiv, 13-31.

1909 *c. 1909-1911:* CHRIST SHOWING HIS HANDS AND HIS FEET TO THOMAS — a terracotta panel, c. 48" (122 cm) square, also designed and executed for the Church of the Mediator.

1911 *c. 1911:* GEORGE TINWORTH — an oval terracotta portrait plaque with the head and shoulders of the sculptor, inscribed on the left-hand side "G. Tinworth" and on the right his monogram.

See Figure 1 for a version of this plaque.

1913 *c. 1909-1913:* CHRIST IN GETHSEMANE — During the last few years of his life, Tinworth suffered increasingly frequent bouts of illness, and his creative powers (already at their zenith by the turn of the century) began to fail more and more noticeably. Although he still produced some notable pieces, the intervals between them increased greatly in the decade before his death in 1913.

He continued to work from time to time on a subject which he had had in mind for many years but had not felt equal to attempting on a large scale, although he had made several sketches and small panels portraying it. This was CHRIST IN GETHSEMANE. The panel, as far as is known, remained in a still unfinished state at the time of Tinworth's death.

In addition to the panels already described, there are a few others to which casual references have been found without any clues to size or date of production, viz:

BALAAM AND THE ASS;

THE GADARENE SWINE;

BY HIS STRIPES YE ARE HEALED;

MESSENGERS COMING TO JOB WITH BAD TIDINGS;

ABRAM AND FAMILY;

THE WISE MEN BEFORE HEROD;

HEALING OF THE SICK;

NICODEMUS COMING TO OUR LORD AT NIGHT;

AFTER THE BAPTISM;

DAVID EATING BREAD AFTER THE DEATH OF HIS SON BY BATHSHEBA;

THE OLD CURIOUSITY SHOP;

MR. PICKWICK PAYING THE CABMAN,

Identification Marks On George Tinworth Pottery and Sculpture

A. Base of Jug (Plate 2) Before 1872. Incised G.T. monogram and "G" with other unidentified initials. Doulton, Lambeth, oval undated mark.

B. Base of Vase (Plate 3A) Before 1872. Incised G.T. monogram on side near base. On base incised "Weir" and unidentified initials. Doulton, Lambeth, oval undated mark. Letter "C" stamp denoting clay type.

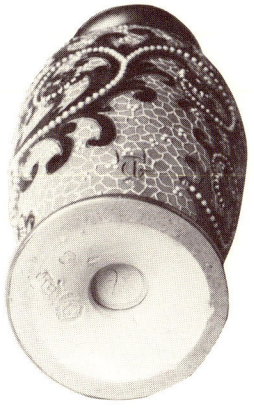

C. Base of Vase (Plate 50B) 1903. Incised G.T. monogram on side near base. On base: Unidentified assistant's mark. Letter "d" in shield, for 1903. Royal Doulton, England, mark.

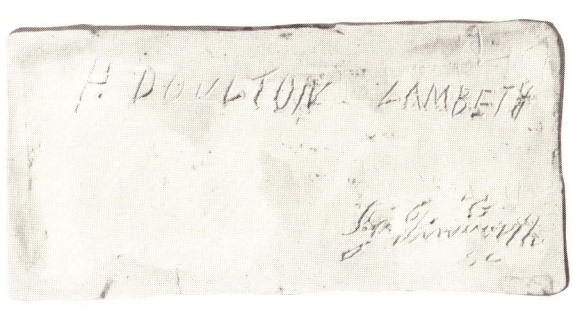

D. Reverse of Plaque (Plate 64) 1871. Incised on reverse: "H. Doulton, Lambeth" and "G. Tinworth Sc." Also G.T. monogram.

E. Bottom edge of Plaque "A word to the Shepherds." Left: incised on lower edge: "H. Doulton & Co. Lambeth" and part of inscription. Right: incised on lower edge: "G. Tinworth". Also G.T. monogram and part of inscription.

Bibliography

A. Books containing sections on, or references to, George Tinworth, or to sculpture and pottery of the period.

BLACKER, J.F.	*The ABC of English Salt-Glaze Stone-Ware from Dwight to Doulton.* Stanley Paul & Co. (London 1922)
	The ABC of XIX Century English Ceramic Art. Stanley Paul & Co. (London 1911)
EYLES, Desmond	*Royal Doulton 1815-1965.* Hutchinson (London 1965)
	The Doulton Lambeth Wares. Hutchinson (London 1975)
	and Richard Dennis *Royal Doulton Figures.* Royal Doulton Tableware Ltd. (Stoke-on-Trent 1978)
GOSSE, Edmund (edited by Desmond Eyles)	*Sir Henry Doulton.* Hutchinson (London 1970)
	A Critical Essay on the Life and Works of George Tinworth. The Fine Art Society (London 1883)
HILLIER, Bevis	*Pottery and Porcelain 1700-1914.* Weidenfeld and Nicolson (London 1968)
JEWITT L. (edited by G.A. Godden)	*Ceramic Art of Great Britain 1800-1900: revised and expanded edition.* Barrie & Jenkins (London 1972)
PROCTOR, John	*The First Hour of the Crucifixion.* An account of the terra cotta panel in the Reredos of St. Stephen's Chapel and of its author George Tinworth 1843-1913. York Minster Picture Books (York undated)
SPARKES, John C.L. and GANDY, Walter	*Potters. Their Arts and Crafts.* Partridge & Co. (London undated)
SPIELMANN, Marion H.	*British Sculpture and Sculptors of Today.* Cassell & Co. (London 1901)
UNDERWOOD, Eric G.	*Short History of English Sculpture.* Faber & Faber (London 1933)
WAKEFIELD, Hugh	*Victorian Pottery.* Herbert Jenkins (London 1962)

B. Articles in contemporary or modern periodicals and journals about, or including references, to George Tinworth.

BLAIKE, J.E.	"The Tinworth Exhibition" *Art Journal New Series.* Vol. 22.	Virtue & Co. London 1883 (pp. 178-10)
DOULTON, Sir Henry	"Random Recollections of a Life" Notes on an address delivered by Sir Henry Doulton at the Doulton Institute, Lambeth on Monday, 3 February, 1896.	*Pottery Bulletin* Doulton & Co. London 1896 (pp. 1-22)
GODDEN, Geoffrey A.	"A Tinworth Diary". Doulton's Ceramic Sculptor.	*Connoisseur* London, December 1968 (pp. 232-234)

HANDLEY-READ, Charles	"Tinworth's Work for Doulton — I" "Sermons in Terra-Cotta"	*Country Life* London, 1 September 1960 (pp. 430-431)
	"Tinworth's Work for Doulton — II" "Salt Cellars and Public Statues"	*Country Life* London, 15 September 1960 (pp. 560, 561)
MONKHOUSE, Cosmo	"Stories in Terra-Cotta" *Magazine of Art.* Vol. 6	Cassell & Co. London June 1883 (pp. 340-344)
ROBJOHNS, Sydney	"Humour in Terra-Cotta: George Tinworth"	*Evangelical Magazine* 1883. (pp. 463-468)
RUSKIN, John	"Notes on some of the Principal Pictures exhibited in the Rooms of the Royal Academy 1975"	*Academy Notes* London 1875 Exhibition Nos. 1293-1295.
SALMON, Edward	"George Tinworth and his Work" *Strand Magazine.* Vol. II.	London 1891 (pp. 442-452)
SPARKES, John	"On some recent inventions and applications of Lambeth stone-ware, terra cotta, and other pottery for internal and external decorations."	Journal Society of Arts Vol. 22. 1 May 1874. (pp. 557-568)
	"On the further development of the fine art section of Lambeth pottery."	Journal Society of Arts Vol. 28. 12 March 1880 (pp. 344-357)
	The substance of the two lectures was published in a booklet, using the title of the first lecture, by Doulton & Co. in 1880.	
WELSH, Rev. R.E.	"The Bible in Terra Cotta"	*Sunday Magazine* London, February 1897. (pp. 92-99)
	"George Tinworth at Work"	*The Young Woman.* London 1895 A Monthly Journal and Review
ANON	"George Tinworth: A record of his work"	Doulton & Co., Lambeth, London 1887.

C. Catalogues and pamphlets, including work by George Tinworth.

ATTERBURY, Paul and IRVINE, Louise	*The Doulton Story* *A Souvenir Booklet produced originally for the exhibition held at the Victoria & Albert Museum, London 1979*	Royal Doulton Tableware Ltd. (Stoke-on-Trent 1979)
BETTERIDGE, Margaret	*Royal Doulton Exhibition 1979*	Museum of Applied Arts & Sciences (Sydney, Australia 1979)
DENNIS, Richard	*Catalogue of an exhibition of Doulton stoneware and terra cotta 1870-1925, Part I.*	Richard Dennis (London, 28 September - 5 July, 1975)
	Catalogue of an exhibition of pottery at The Fine Art Society: Doulton Pottery from the Lambeth and Burslem Studios 1873-1939, Part II.	Richard Dennis (London, 24 June - 5 July, 1975)

EDWARDS, Rhoda	*Lambeth Stoneware.: The Woolley Collection, including Doulton Ware and products of other British potteries.*	London Borough of Lambeth (London, 1973)
HANDLEY-READ, Lavinia	*Introduction to catalogue British Sculpture 1850-1914.*	The Fine Art Society (London 1968)
ROYAL DOULTON POTTERIES		
	Sculpture in Terra Cotta by George Tinworth, 1890.	Doulton & Co. Ltd. Lambeth (London 1890)
	Catalogue of an exhibition of the works of Mr. George Tinworth.	Held at the premises of Messrs. Doulton & Co. Lambeth, (London c. 1896/97)

D. Manuscript and other unpublished material, and ephemera.

The Southwark Local Studies Library, Southwark, London contains a collection of Tinworth letters, newspaper articles and photographs collected together in the early 1900's by the Librarian, Richard W. Mould. It also holds the manuscript autobiography of Tinworth "The Life Story of George Tinworth, Wheelwright and Sculptor" told by himself, written 1911-1913.

The Royal Doulton Tableware Ltd. archive contains a large collection of photographs of works by George Tinworth, and pamphlets, booklets etc. issued by Doulton & Co. at various times. It also holds the manuscript of Mrs. Tinworth's Diary for 1888 and a typescript of a lecture given by John Shorter Senior "George Tinworth, the Sculptor Preacher" (circa 1914).

The Edmund Gosse archive in the Brotherton Library, Leeds University, contains several letters written by Tinworth to Gosse. A small number of issues of "Studio Notes" have survived in private collections. These were issued initially six times, and then four times a year, over a period of approximately ten years in the 1880s and early 1890s. They consisted of original drawings, paintings and handwritten articles by Doulton Artists, bound together in book form and circulated to subscribers in the firm. There are a number of references to Tinworth in them.

Index

Works by George Tinworth which appear exclusively in either the Catalogue or in the Chronology of Principal Works are not indexed. Works which are referred to elsewhere in the text are, however, indexed: in these cases the Catalogue and the Chronology references are included where appropriate. Colour plate numbers are printed in bold type; the page numbers of black and white illustrations appear in italics.

Agony in Gethsemane (c. 1895), 46
All Misery Past, 47, 48
    See also Sunset to Sunset
America, (Doulton & Co. interest in), 26
Anthropomorphism, 56, 76
Architect, The, 33
Art Journal, The, 26, 55

Ball, Percy, 16
Barlow, Arthur, 24, 160
Barlow, Florence, 24
Barlow, Hannah, 24, 160
Barlow, Lucy, 24
Bell, John, 159
Brighton (visits to by G.T.), 38
British Late 19th Century Sculpture, 55
Blaikie, J.A., 33, 35
Butler, Frank, 24, 58, 160

Carroll, Lewis (Rev. Dodson), 56
Casting out of the Money-Lenders, The, 24, 74, 157, **66**
Centennial Exhibition, Philadelphia
    See Philadelphia
Central Government Art School, South Kensington
    Later Royal College of Art, 18
Chadwick, Edwin, *later* Sir Edwin
    sanitary reforms, 21
    conversations with G.T., 36
    description of bust, 173
Chicago, World Fair (1893), 40, 58, 180
Christ before Herod (1887), 46, 176, *176*
Cockneys at Brighton (1886), 56, **104**
Country Life, 52, 55
Cresy, Edward, 21, 22
Cuming Museum, 50

David with the head of Goliath (1876), 28, 159
De Morgan, William, 22, 35
Digweed, Ellen, 50
Doulton and Company: "Limited" from
  1899; prefix "Royal" from 1901.
    establishment of Art Pottery, 21, 22
    appointment of artist assistants, 24
    publication of pamphlet on G.T., 40
    publication of *From Sunset to Sunset*, 47-48
    marking of pottery, 63
Doulton, Henry, *later* Sir Henry
    friendship with John Sparkes, 18
    establishment of Art Pottery, 21-22
    decision to exhibit G.T.'s work, 31
    "The Big Potter", 35
    liking for animal groups, 76
    lecture at Royal Institute, 38
    fire at pottery, 38
    commission of monument, 40
    death, 41, 45
    donation of fountain, 155
    portrayal of, 160, *43*
    presentation of panel by G.T., 171
    visit to country residence by G.T., 177
    memorial presentation of panels by G.T., 184
Doulton, Henry Lewis (son of H.D.), 81, 84, **130, 152**

Doulton, James (cousin of H.D.), 24-25
Doulton, John (father of H.D.), 21, 24, 155
Exhibitions
    International Exhibition, London (1862), 22
    International Exhibition, Paris (1867), 24
    Centennial Exhibition, Philadelphia (1876), 26, 28, 40, 58, 158, 159, 160
    International Exhibition, Paris (1878), 31
    Conduit St., London (1883), 12
    International Health Exhibition, London (1884), 35
    Jubilee Exhibition, Manchester (1887), 35
    International Exhibition, Glasgow (1888), 35
    World's Fair, Chicago (1893), 40
Eyles, Desmond, 12, 24

Fairhall, Walter, 46
Fawcett, Professor Henry (monument to, 1891-1892), 40, 59, 179, *41*
Fine Art Society, 55, 74, 157
Foley, John Henry, R.A., 19
Football Scrimmage, The (1876), 30, 154
Fountain (1878), 31, 58, 161, *32*
Four Seasons, The
    See Seasons
French Academy (G.T. officer of), 11
From Sunset to Sunset
    See Sunset

Genesis (1886), 36, 174
Going to Calvary (1879), 61, 164, *165*
Going to the Derby and its pair (c. 1885), 56, **120, 121**
Gosse, Edmund, *later* Sir Edmund
    description of plaster group by G.T., 22
    views on early salt-glaze panels, 24
    criticism of *The Football Scrimmage,* 31
    views on York Minster Reredos, 161
    criticism of *Fountain,* 31
    catalogue for Conduit St. Exhibition, 12, 31
    presentation of panel by G.T., 36, 170-171
    death of H.D., 41
    unveiling of panel, 50
    articles on *New Sculpture,* 55
    attitude of G.T. to human body, 57
Gower, Lord Ronald, 30
Greek Mother, The (1904-1906), 49, 186, *49*
Gregory, Canon, 18, *17*
Gres de Flandres, 21, 58
Grosvenor Gallery exhibitions, 36
Guards' Chapel
    See Royal Military

Handel (bust of 1861), 16, 50, 154
Handley-Read, Charles, 52, 55, 56, 58, 59
Handley-Read, Lavinia, 55
Harriman-Judd collection, 28, 30, 31, 40, 56, 58
Hercules (medallion 1867-1868), 22, 155, *23*
History of England vase (1892-1893), 40, 58, 179, **52, 53, 54, 55**
Hollowell, William, 47

Illustrated London News, The, 33
International exhibitions
    See Exhibitions

Jews Making Bricks in Egypt, The (1892-1896), 50, 182
Jubilee Exhibition, Manchester (1887), 35
Judgment of Solomon, The (undated), 46

Lambeth School of Art, 16
Landseer, Sir Edwin R.A., 56
Louvre Museum, Paris, 26

Magazine of Art, The, 55

Marshall, Mark V., 35, 58
Martin Brothers, 58
    See also individually
Martin, Edwin, 24
Martin, Robert Wallace
    friendship with G.T., 16
        attitude to graded tests and prizes, 18
        funeral of G.T., 52
        Martin Birds, 56
Martin, Walter, 24
Morley College lunette (1888), 39, 59, 178, *40*
Moses (1884), 36,
Mould, Richard W., 49-50
Musicians Merry, also Boy Musicians, 48, 57, 83, **146, 147, 148, 149**

Newington Public Library (exhibition at), 50
Noah Constructing his Ark (1895-1897), 46, 183, *47*

Paul Entering Rome, (1897-1902), 45, 184
Peace and Wrath in Low Life (1866), 22, 154
People, The, 33
Philadelphia Centennial Exhibition (1876), 26, 28, 40, 58, 158, 159, 160
Playgoers, 56, **112**
Pottery Gazette, 46
Preparing for the Crucifixion (1881-1882), 31, 52, 166

Release of Barabbas, The (1875), 27, 31, 46, 157
Remorse of Herod (undated), 49
Reredos, York Minster
    See York Minster
Royal Academy, 21, 26, 28, 30, 31, 36, 154, 164, 165, 166, 170
Royal Academy Schools, 18, 19
Royal Military Chapel (Guard's Chapel), London, 30, 60, 159, *30*
    maquettes for, 71, 74, **69-85**
Ruskin, John
    admired by Henry Doulton, 21
    critical attention drawn to G.T., 27
    admiration for and visit to G.T., 30
    effect of advocacy of bas-relief, 36, 59-60

Salmon, Edward, 76
Seasons, The Four (1876), 30, 57, 85, 160, **160A & B, 161A & B**
Sevres Museum, Paris, 26
Sex, G.T.'s attitude to, 57
Shaftesbury Memorial panel (1888), 38, 59, 177, *39*
Shakespeare Memorial (1904-1906), 49, 50, 186, *51, 187*
Shorter, John (Senior), 48, 49
Society of Arts, London, *later* Royal, 28, 58
Sons of Cydippe, The, 36, 49, 72, 170, **58, 59, 60**
Southwark Central Library, 50
Sowing of Tares, The (1878), 30, 74, 163, *164*
Sparkes, John C.L.
    meeting with G.T., 16
    teaching at Lambeth, 18
    later career, 18
    generosity to G.T., 19
    establishment of Art Pottery, 21-22
    design of fountain, 24, 155
    Society of Arts lectures, 28
    design for an exhibition pavilion, 35
    choice of lunette for book, 40
    G.T.'s sense of pattern, 58
Spielmann, Marion H., 55, 59, 60
Spurgeon, Rev. Charles Hadden (memorial 1894), 40-41, 59, 182, *42*
Stacy-Marks, Henry R.A., 21
Strand Magazine, The, 30, 74, 159
Street, George Edmund 30, 74, 159
Sunday at Home, 177

Sunday Magazine, 46
Sunset to Sunset, From (1900-1907), 47-48, 185, *48*
Swimming Bath, The (undated), 57, 82, **137, 138, 139**

Tambourine Player (undated), 57, **154**
Tenniel, John, 56
The Times (obituary of G.T.), 52-53
Tinworth, Alice, *nee* Digweed (wife of G.T.)
    letter to Gosse, 12
    sale of large panel, 36, 165
    diary, 37-39, 79, *37*
    illness, 50
Tinworth, George (1843-1913)
    birth, 12
    childhood, 11
    poverty, 13, 14
    loss of wheelbarrow, 14
    purchase of china figures, 14
    Christmas puddings, 14
    first job in fireworks factory, 15
    Lambeth School of Art, 16
    friendship with R.W. Martin, 16, 18
    Royal Academy Schools, 18, 19
    failure in gold medal competition, 19
    death of father, 22
    offer of job at Doulton & Co., 22
    visit to France (1873), 25
    identification with children, 31
    Conduit St.Exhibition (1883), 12, 31
    officer of the French Academy (1876), 11, 45, 61
    cost of G.T.'s studio, 35
    gratitude to Gosse, 36, 170
    experiement with painting, 38
    visits to Brighton, 38
    fire at pottery, 38
    visit to Rome, 45
    Shakespeare Memorial project, 50, *51*
    autobiography, 50
    marks on sculpture & pottery, 63
    decoration of pottery, 64, 65
    lemonade jugs, 66
    religious panels, 71
    animal groups, 76
    human figures, 82
    death, 51
Tinworth, Jane, *nee* Daniel (mother of G.T.), 13
Tinworth, Joshua (father of G.T.)
    the slater's practical joke, 13
    failure of business, 14
    unquenched pride, 14
    imitation pistol, 16
    death, 22
Tinworth, Thomas (brother of G.T.), 18, 50, 154

Underwood, Eric, 55

Wales, Edward & Alexandra, Prince & Princess of
    later Edward VIII & Queen Alexandra, 31, 33, 35, 38, 170
Walsh, Rev. R.E., 45-46
Way, Sir Samuel, 49
Weekes, Henry, R.A., 19
Wheelwright's Shop, The (1877), 15, 30, 50, 161, *15*
Wise and the Foolish, The (1871-1873), 24, 74, 157
Wise Men opening their Treasures, The (1902), 46, 184
World's Fair, Chicago
    See Exhibitions

York Minster, *Reredos* (1876), 30, 159, 161, *30*
Young Woman, The, 46